THE YEAR YOU WERE BO
1962

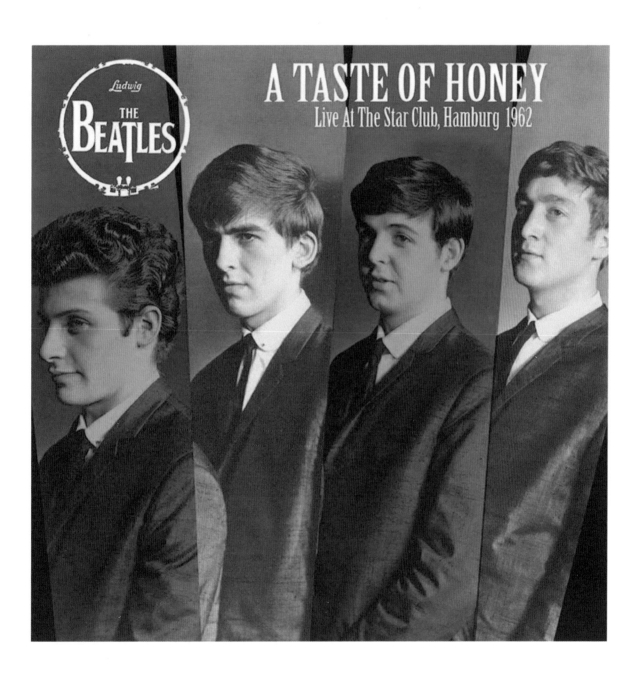

A fascinating book about the year 1962 with information on:
Events of the year UK, Adverts of 1962, Cost of living, Births, Sporting events,
Book publications, Movies, Music, World events and People in power.

INDEX

UK EVENTS OF 1962

1st An outbreak of smallpox starts spreading from Cardiff and infects 45 people and kills 19 in south Wales; 900,000 people in the region are vaccinated against the disease.

2nd BBC Television broadcasts the first episode of Z-Cars, noted as a realistic portrayal of the police.

5th the first album on which The Beatles play, My Bonnie, credited to "Tony Sheridan and the Beat Brothers" (recorded last June in Hamburg), is released by Polydor.

7th The UK was blanketed with snow in an unusual winter storm. Overnight temperatures of −18 °C (0 °F) were recorded during the morning at Benson, Oxfordshire and Woodford, Greater Manchester in Britain.

11th An outbreak of smallpox in Bradford in 1962 first came to attention on the 11th January 1962, when a cook from the children's hospital in Bradford, West Riding of Yorkshire, England, presented with an unexplained fever and was found to have changes in her blood similar to another sick person at the nearby St Luke's Hospital, both samples appearing compatible with smallpox. The index case was later discovered to be a nine-year old girl who arrived in the UK on the 16th December 1961 from Karachi, Pakistan, where there was an ongoing epidemic of smallpox.

15th After the United Kingdom sought to join the European Economic Community, the Meteorological Office first began using Celsius temperature values in its public weather information, following the Fahrenheit values. In October, the Celsius values were listed first, and by 1st January 1973, when the government entered the EEC and completed its conversion to the metric system, Fahrenheit numbers were only used occasionally.

18th Union-Castle Line ship RMS Transvaal Castle (1961) makes her maiden voyage Southampton–Durban, perhaps the last major British ship built to enter the regular passenger ocean liner trade.

20th Petula Clark had her first number one hit in France with "Romeo".

22nd James Hanratty goes on trial for the A6 murder. He denies the murder of 36-year-old Michael Gregsten and the attempted murder of Mr Gregsten's mistress Valerie Storie, who is paralysed by a gunshot wound.

January

24th | Brian Epstein made a verbal contract with the four members of The Beatles, becoming their manager in return for receiving up to 25 percent of their gross earnings.

February

2nd | The last underground shift was worked at the colliery in Radcliffe, Northumberland.

4th | The Sunday Times becomes the first newspaper to print a colour supplement.

5th | Hours before the Beatles were scheduled to play at the Cavern Club, drummer Pete Best told his fellow musicians that he was ill and wouldn't be able to appear. Determined not to cancel the show, the group called around for a replacement and Ringo Starr, whose group had the day off, appeared in Best's place.

8th | The British government announced that it would grant independence to Jamaica effective 6th August 19...

10th | The end of the Queen's 10th regnal year. From this year, Acts of Parliament are dated by calendar year.

11th | The UK selects its entry for the 1962 Eurovision Song Contest from a shortlist of 12. The winner is "Ring-ding Girl" sung by Ronnie Carroll.

12th | The body of British aviator Bill Lancaster was discovered almost 29 years after he had disappeared over the Sahara in the Southern Cross Minor. Lancaster had last been seen on the 12th April 1933, when he to... off from Reggane in French Algeria.

17th | After being rejected by both her lover, Richard Burton, and her husband, Eddie Fisher, actress Elizabeth Taylor attempted suicide by taking an overdose of Seconal sleeping pills. She was saved after being rush... to the Salvator Mundi Hospital in Rome, where she and Burton were filming Cleopatra. The 20th Centur... Fox studio invented a cover story that Taylor had become seriously ill from food poisoning.

21st | Margot Fonteyn and Rudolf Nureyev first danced together, in a Royal Ballet performance of Giselle at Covent Garden in London, creating one of the greatest partnerships in the history of dance. Nureyev had defected from the U.S.S.R. almost eight months earlier on the 16th June 1961. He and Fonteyn received ... curtain calls from the audience.

ROYAL
BALLET

th The Irish Republican Army officially called off its five-year Border Campaign in Northern Ireland. In press releases dropped off at newspapers there as well as in Ireland, the IRA publicity bureau wrote, "The Leadership of the Resistance Movement has ordered the termination of 'The Campaign of Resistance to British Occupation'... all arms and other materials have been dumped and all full-time active service volunteers have been withdrawn." With the exception of a series of 17 bank robberies to finance the organization, the IRA violence halted until 1969.

th The United Kingdom's House of Commons voted 277-170 in favour of the Commonwealth Immigrants Act 1962, designed to limit the immigration into Great Britain by residents of India, Pakistan, and the West Indies.

th The Beatles appeared at the Cavern Club in Liverpool on a triple bill with Gerry & the Pacemakers and Johnny Sandon and the Searchers.

arch

1st British nuclear testing in the United States begins with "Pampas", Britain's first underground test, at the Nevada Test Site, the first of 24 critical tests up to 1991.

rd The United Kingdom designated all land south of 60°S latitude and between longitudes 20°W and 80°W as the British Antarctic Territory, making a claim to an area of 1,710,000 square kilometres or 660,000 square miles. In addition to the wedge of the Antarctic continent, the territory included the uninhabited South Orkney Islands and the South Shetland Islands, while putting South Georgia and the South Sandwich Islands under the jurisdiction of the Falkland Islands. The claim to the territories was not recognized by Argentina.

th In London, the Royal College of Physicians issued its report, "Smoking and Health", declaring that "Cigarette smoking is a cause of lung cancer. It also causes bronchitis and probably contributes to the development of coronary heart disease and various other less common diseases. It delays healing of gastric and duodenal ulcers." Sir Robert Platt, the president of the organization, led a committee of nine physicians to compile the research. A panel led by the U.S. Surgeon General would draw a similar conclusion nearly two years later on the 11th January 1964.

th The Beatles made their radio debut, with a three-song session, recorded the day before, and broadcast on the BBC Manchester programme Teenager's Turn (Here We Go). They performed the songs "Dream Baby (How Long Must I Dream)", "Please Mr. Postman", and "Memphis, Tennessee".

th Kilmarnock F.C.'s home attendance record was broken when a crowd of 35,995 turned out to see them play Glasgow Rangers in the Scottish Cup, at the Rugby Park stadium.

th A by-election is held in Blackpool North: the seat is retained by the Conservatives. This is the last parliamentary by-election in England to be held on a day other than Thursday.

th The annual Gaelic Games competition was televised for the first time, as RTÉ broadcast the finals of the Railway Cup, hurling championship of the Gaelic Athletic Association. Leinster beat defending champion Munster by a score of 1 goal, 11 points to 1 goal, nine points, equivalent to 14–12.

March

21st   English actor Rex Harrison married Welsh actress Rachel Roberts. The two Britons were wed in a civil ceremony in Italy at Genoa.

29th   Education Act 1962 requires local education authorities to pay the tuition fees of students attending full time first degree (or comparable) courses and to provide them with a maintenance grant, superseding the former system of State Scholarships.

April

2nd   Panda crossings are introduced but their complex sequences of pulsating and flashing lights cause confusion amongst drivers and pedestrians. The first public example was opened on the 2nd April of that year outside London Waterloo railway station. The majority of the initial sites used for this experiment were in Guildford where all thirteen existing crossings were converted, and in Lincoln where ten crossings were converted. By 1967 the panda crossing was a matter of concern for the Ministry of Transport, and a new type of crossing, the X-way, was introduced. The new system was not phased in gradually by replacement; rather the pandas were removed seemingly as a matter of urgency. The replacement was urgent that although the X-way lights replaced the panda crossing lights, the road initially retained the black-and-white triangular markings until they could be removed at a later date. The X-way itself soon disappeared when, in 1969, the modern-day pelican crossing was introduced.

4th   James Hanratty was hanged in Bedford Gaol for the 1961 A6 murder. Afterward, witnesses came forward to testify that they had seen him in another town at the time. In 1997, a police committee would conclude that he had been wrongfully convicted, but the decision was reversed by the Criminal Cases Review Commission, and upheld by a court of appeal in 2002.

7th At the Ealing Jazz Club in London, Brian Jones was introduced to Mick Jagger and Keith Richards. The three would become the heart of The Rolling Stones, formed later that year.

9th Jamaica held its first parliamentary elections, in preparation for its independence from the United Kingdom. The Jamaica Labour Party won 26 of 45 parliamentary seats, making Alexander Bustamante the new Prime Minister. Losing its legislative majority was the People's National Party, led by colonial Chief Minister Norman Manley.

7th In a by-election for the UK parliamentary constituency of Derby North, caused by the death of sitting MP Clifford Wilcock, Niall MacDermot retained the seat for the Labour Party.

8th The Commonwealth Immigrants Act in the United Kingdom received royal assent, removing free immigration from the citizens of member states of the Commonwealth of Nations, requiring proof of employment in the UK. The law would go into effect on the 1st July.

3rd At a motor racing meeting at Goodwood Circuit, UK, Graham Hill won the 1962 Glover Trophy and Bruce McLaren won the 1962 Lavant Cup. During the Glover Trophy race, Stirling Moss suffered serious injuries in an accident, which effectively ended his career as a top-level racing driver.

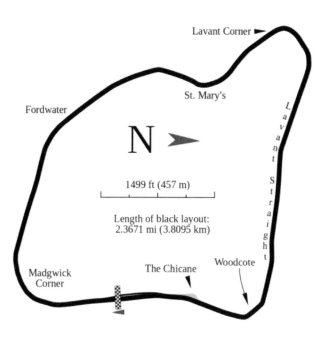

6th The first British satellite, Ariel 1, was launched at 1800 UTC from the Wallops Flight Facility in the United States, and remained in Earth orbit until the 24th April 1976. The United Kingdom and United States collaboration made the launch the first multinational space effort in history.

8th Ipswich Town F.C. finished in first place in the English League, winning the league championship with a record of 24 wins, 8 draws and 10 losses. The team was in its first season in the soccer football league's First Division, having been promoted from Second Division play after its 1960–61 finish. It was the first time since 1889 that the major league championship was captured by a first year team. Dundee F.C. won its first Scottish League title on the same day, with a record of 25-4-5.

May

1st   Norwich City F.C. won the English Football League Cup, beating Rochdale F.C. in the final.

3rd   British supermarket executive Alan Sainsbury was created a life peer.

5th   Tottenham Hotspur F.C. retained the FA Cup with a 3–1 win over Burnley F.C. in front of 100,000 fans (including Queen Elizabeth II and Prince Philip) at Wembley Stadium, and became only the second team Football League history to win the Cup two years in a row. Goals were scored for the Spurs by Jimmy Greaves, Bobby Smith and captain Danny Blanchflower, with the Clarets' sole score coming from Jimmy Robson.

8th   The last trolleybuses in London run. Trolleybuses served the London Passenger Transport Area from 193 until 1962. For much of its existence, the London system was the largest in the world. It peaked at 68 routes, with a maximum fleet of 1,811 trolleybuses.

8th   Brian Epstein visited the HMV (EMI) store at 363 Oxford Street, London, to have The Beatles' Decca audition tape transferred to 78 rpm acetates.

9th   The Beatles signed their first recording contract, with Parlophone, after Brian Epstein persuaded George Martin to sign them, sight unseen.

18th   British soldiers erected a barbed wire barricade along Hong Kong's 12-mile border with the People's Republic of China. The purpose was to block refugees from fleeing China into Hong Kong. At the time, as many as 4,000 people were attempting to flee Communist China into the British colony. The next day, British administrators imposed penalties on any Hong Kong resident attempting to assist a refugee's escape.

20th   The 1962 Dutch Grand Prix at Circuit Park Zandvoort opened the Formula One Championship season. It was won by Graham Hill. The non-championship 1962 Naples Grand Prix took place on the same day at t Posillipo Circuit, and was won by Willy Mairesse.

31st   The Northern Ireland general election produced a large majority for the Ulster Unionist Party, which wor 34 out of 51 seats. The Nationalist Party gained 2 seats to give it a total of nine.

nd | Britain's first legal casino opens in Brighton, Sussex.

4th | The 1962 Isle of Man TT races were held at the Snaefell Mountain Course. Winners included Luigi Taveri, Derek Minter and Ernst Degner.

5th | The Beatles first auditioned for record producer George Martin at the Abbey Road Studios.

8th | Sir Alfred Dudley Ward became Governor of Gibraltar.

1th | Following a successful pilot episode shown in January, the classic British sitcom Steptoe and Son began its 12-year run on BBC. Described as "the most popular situation comedy in British television history", the series about junk dealer Albert Steptoe (Wilfrid Bramble) and his son Harold (Harry H. Corbett) would later inspired an American counterpart, Sanford and Son.

5th | On the death of his father, Viscount Hinchingbrooke succeeded to the earldom of Sandwich, obliging him to give up his seat in the British House of Commons.

6th | English cricketer Geoffrey Boycott began his 24-year professional career, appearing for the Yorkshire County Cricket Club.

7th | In the UK, British Railways closed the former South Eastern Railway motive power depot at Bricklayers Arms in London, after 118 years in operation.

7th | The Pilkington Committee on Broadcasting publishes its report, recommending that the BBC should extend its activities to the creation of local radio stations to forestall the introduction of commercial radio. In 1962 the BBC runs a series of closed circuit experiments in local radio from a variety of locations across England.

0th | Unrestricted immigration, of British Empire subjects, to the United Kingdom was curtailed as the Commonwealth Immigrants Act 1962 took effect, putting a quota on how many government vouchers would be issued for each nation. Restrictions would become stricter in 1971

1st | Another heavy smog develops over London.

July

3rd Opening of Chichester Festival Theatre, Britain's first large modern theatre with a thrust stage. Laurence Olivier is the first artistic director.

6th Irish broadcaster Gay Byrne presented his first edition of The Late Late Show. Byrne would go on to present the talk show for 37 years making Byrne the longest running TV talk show host in history.

11th The first person to swim across the English Channel underwater, without surfacing, arrived in Sandwich Bay at Dover 18 hours after departing from Calais. Fred Baldasare wore scuba gear and was assisted by a guiding ship in the use of oxygen tanks.

12th The Rolling Stones made their debut at London's Marquee Club, Number 165 Oxford Street, opening for the first time under that name, for Long John Baldry. Mick Jagger, Brian Jones, Keith Richards, Ian Stewart Dick Taylor and Tony Chapman had played together for the group Blues Incorporated before creating a new name inspired by the Muddy Waters 1950 single "Rollin' Stone". The day before the concert, an ad in the 11th July 1962 edition of Jazz News, a London weekly jazz paper, had showed the drummer to be Mick Avory, who later played for The Kinks, rather than Chapman. Avory himself, however, would say in an interview that he did not play in the event.

13th With his popularity declining, British Prime Minister Harold Macmillan fired seven senior members of his cabinet, including Chancellor of the Exchequer Selwyn Lloyd, the Lord Chancellor, the Ministers of Defence and Education, and the Secretary of State for Scotland. The move was unprecedented in United Kingdom history, and was followed by the firing of nine junior ministers on Monday. Liberal MP Jeremy Thorpe would quip, "Greater love hath no man than this that he lay down his friends for his life." The British press would dub the event Macmillan's "Night of the Long Knives".

14th In the third match of the rugby league Test series between Australia and Great Britain, held at Sydney Cricket Ground, a controversial last-minute Australian try and the subsequent conversion resulted in an 18–17 win for Australia.

20th The world's first regular passenger hovercraft service was introduced, as the VA-3 began the 20-mile run between Rhyl (in Wales) and Wallasey (in England).

3rd Telstar relayed the first live trans-Atlantic television signal, with two 20-minute programs. The first was a set of U.S. TV shows (President Kennedy's news conference, 90 seconds of the Phillies-Cubs baseball game, and the Mormon Tabernacle Choir) to Eurovision (2:00 pm New York, 8:00 pm London). At 4:58 pm, New York Time, live transmission of European broadcasting was shown on all three American networks, beginning with a live picture of the clock at London's Big Ben approaching 11:00 pm.

4th The first successful use of a biological valve in human heart surgery was performed by Dr. Donald Nixon Ross in London, with a sub coronary implantation of an aortic allograft.

5th Buckingham Palace, residence of the Queen of the United Kingdom, was opened to the public for the first time with the dedication of the Queen's Gallery, an art museum.

8th Race riots broke out in Dudley, West Midlands, UK.

9th Sir Oswald Mosley, who had founded the British Union of Fascists and been a vocal Nazi sympathizer prior to Germany's attack on Britain in World War Two, was beaten by an angry crowd in Manchester, after leading members of his extreme right-wing Union Movement on a march through the city.

gust

1st In the UK, the Tenbury and Bewdley Railway was closed to passengers, under the cutbacks of the Beeching Axe.

4th Cymdeithas yr Iaith Gymraeg, the Welsh Language Society, is founded.

5th Graham Hill won the 1962 German Grand Prix at the Nürburgring.

6th Jamaica became independent. Princess Margaret of the United Kingdom and U.S Vice-President Lyndon Johnson were among the dignitaries who watched the lowering of the British flag in Kingston.

2th The BMC ADO16 economy car series, best known as the Austin/Morris 1100, is launched; this becomes Britain's best-selling car for most of the 1960s.

August

16th | Beatles drummer Pete Best was fired and replaced by Ringo Starr.

17th | The Tornados' recording of Joe Meek's "Telstar" is released. The Tornados were an English instrumental group of the 1960s that acted as backing group for many of record producer Joe Meek's productions and also for singer Billy Fury. They enjoyed several chart hits in their own right, including the UK and U.S. No "Telstar" (named after the satellite and composed and produced by Meek), the first U.S. No. 1 single by British group.

18th | The Beatles play their first live engagement with the line-up of John, Paul, George and Ringo, at Hulme Hall, Port Sunlight.

23rd | John Lennon secretly married Cynthia Powell at Mount Pleasant Register office in Liverpool. Lennon's fellow Beatles, Paul McCartney and George Harrison, attended the ceremony, and their manager Brian Epstein was best man.

31st | Mountaineers Chris Bonington and Ian Clough becomes the first Britons to climb the north face of the Eiger.

September

1st | Channel Television, the ITV franchise for the Channel Islands, goes on air. ITV Channel Television, previously Channel Television, is a British television station which has served as the ITV contractor for the Channel Islands since 1962. It is based in Jersey and broadcasts regional programme for insertion into the network ITV schedule.

2nd | Glasgow Corporation Tramways runs its last cars in normal service, leaving the Blackpool tramway as the only remaining one in Britain.

4th | The Beatles made their first recording of a song that would become a hit single, "Love Me Do". It would become their fourth #1 song in the United States, in 1964.

6th | The first of the "Blackfriars Ships" was discovered by archaeologist Peter Marsden in London, buried in the mud of the Thames River and literally "under the shadow of Blackfriars Bridge". With a cofferdam to hold back the waters during low tide, and assistance from the London Fire Brigade, the oak craft was excavated. From pottery shards in the wreckage, Marsden estimated that the ship sank during the 2nd century AD, when Britain was ruled by the Roman Empire.

7th The Buckfastleigh, Totnes and South Devon Railway, in England, were closed by the Western Region of British Railways.

9th The railroad line between Taunton and Chard Junction, within Somerset, became the first casualty of the "Beeching cuts" after the Chairman of British Railways, Richard Beeching, began shutting down unprofitable railroad lines. For the next 13 years, passenger service would be halted permanently at 29 separate rail routes, a process accelerated after the publishing of the "Beeching Report" on March 27, 1963. An author would note later that 4,500 miles of routes, 2,500 stations, and 67,700 jobs would be ended the closures.

8th The last Gentlemen v Players cricket match played, at Scarborough.

14th Teledu Cymru (now Wales West and North Television) began broadcasting to the North and West Wales region of Britain, extending the ITV Network to the whole of the United Kingdom. Transmitters were located at Pembroke, Caernarvon and Flint.

17th BBC Wales Today was broadcast for the first time. As of September 17, 2012, it will have been on the air for fifty years as one of the world's longest-running daily television news programmes.

9th Ford launches the Cortina, a family saloon costing £573 and similar in size to the Vauxhall Victor, Hillman Minx and Morris Oxford Farina.

1st First broadcast of the long-running television quiz programme University Challenge, made by Granada Television with Bamber Gascoigne as quizmaster.

The British music magazine New Musical Express published a story about two 13-year-old schoolgirls, "Sue" and "Mary", releasing a disc on Decca, and added that "A Liverpool group, The Beatles, have recorded 'Love Me Do' for Parlophone Records, set for October 5 release."

tober

1st Elizabeth Lane takes her seat as the first female county court judge.

October

5th | Dr No, the first James Bond film, is premiered at the London Pavilion, with 32-year-old Edinburgh-born Sean Connery playing the lead, a British Secret Service agent.

The Beatles' first single in Love Me Do, is released by Parlophone. This version was recorded on the 4th September at Abbey Road Studios in London with Ringo Starr as drummer.

16th | The Beatles make their first televised appearance, on Granada television's local news programme People and Places.

17th | The British International Motor Show opened at Earl's Court in London. The Triumph Spitfire was among new vehicles showcased during the event.

21st | The first American Folk Blues Festival European tour plays its only UK date at the Free Trade Hall, Manchester; artists include Sonny Terry, Brownie McGhee and T-Bone Walker. It will be influential on the British R&B scene, with the audience including Mick Jagger, Keith Richards and Brian Jones of The Rolling Stones with Jimmy Page, Paul Jones, John Mayall and other musicians, and with a second show filmed and shown on Independent Television.

22nd | Manchester Ringway Airport opens the first hub and pier terminal in Europe.

24th | GCHQ's interception station at Scarborough is the first to detect that Soviet merchant ships implicated in the Cuban Missile Crisis are returning to their bases.

28th | The ferry SS Lisieux caught fire on a voyage between Newhaven, East Sussex (UK) and Dieppe (France), and was escorted into Dieppe at reduced speed.

29th | The British airline East Anglian Flying Services was renamed Channel Airways.

31st | The UN General Assembly asks the United Kingdom to suspend enforcement of the new constitution in Southern Rhodesia (now Zimbabwe), but the constitution comes into effect on 1st November.

November

6th | The United Nations General Assembly passed a resolution condemning South Africa's racist apartheid policies, and called for all UN member states to cease military and economic relations with the nation. The result was 67 in favour, 16 against (including the U.S., the U.K., France, Japan, Canada, New Zealand and South Africa), and 27 abstaining.

11th | The French ship Jean Gougy ran aground at Land's End, Cornwall, United Kingdom and capsized. Eight of the twenty crew were rescued by helicopter or breeches buoy. Sergeant Eric Smith of 22 Squadron, Royal Air Force would be awarded a George Medal for his actions in the rescue.

17th | The Seaham life-boat George Elmey capsized while entering harbour after rescuing the crew of a fishing boat. All five crew and four of the five survivors were killed.

22nd | The Chippenham by-election, caused by previous MP David Eccles, having been raised to the House of Lords, was won by Daniel Awdry of the Conservative Party.

4th The first episode of influential British satire show That Was The Week That Was was broadcast on BBC Television.

5th The Beatles made their definitive recording of "Please Please Me" at EMI Studios in London. George Martin produces.

9th An agreement is signed between Britain and France to develop the Concorde supersonic airliner.

cember

1st The 1962 British Empire and Commonwealth Games came to an end, in Perth, Western Australia.

2nd A week of severe smog began in London, killing at least 106 people over four days, and causing the hospitalization of over 1,000. Most of the persons whose deaths were blamed on the fog had had pre-existing heart and lung problems, with 66 dead in the first three days. In 1952, at least 4,000 people had been killed over nine days by the combination of factory pollution and fog.

4th The first Jacob's Awards ceremony was held in Dublin, marking the first awards for achievement in Irish television. Winners included Joe Lynch, Charles Mitchel and Proinsias Mac Aonghusa.

5th The first Test match of the 1962–63 Ashes series ended in a draw at Brisbane Cricket Ground.

7th Bill Wyman was hired as bass player in The Rolling Stones.

9th A year after it had become independent from the United Kingdom, Tanganyika (now Tanzania) became a republic within the Commonwealth, with Prime Minister Julius Nyerere becoming President, and Richard Gordon Turnbull ending his term as the only Governor-General of Tanganyika. Nyerere would continue as President after the nation's merger with Zanzibar, retiring on the 5th November 1985.

0th Scottish boxer Jackie Brown defeated Nigeria's Orizu Obilaso to win the Commonwealth flyweight title.

4th Hugh Gaitskell, the Leader of the Opposition in the United Kingdom as head of the Labour Party, first showed the symptoms of Lupus erythematosus, from which he would die 25 days later at the age of 56. Because the illness came the day after Gaitskell had visited the Soviet Embassy in London to have tea, and Soviet journals had described a drug that could cause systemic lupus, conspiracy theorists suggested a link between the two events. The Labour Party would win a majority two years later after Gaitskell's death at the age of 56.

1st At a meeting between British Prime Minister Harold Macmillan and U.S. President John F. Kennedy in the Bahamas at Nassau, the United Kingdom agreed to purchase Polaris missiles from the United States, to replace the British-made Skybolt missiles. The Macmillan government was heavily criticized by the opposition, with accusations that he had sacrificed Britain's "nuclear independence" with no apparent gain.

2nd For the first time, a song by a British band reached #1 on the American singles chart. More than a year before The Beatles began music's "British Invasion", the instrumental song "Telstar" became a hit for The Tornados.

December

22nd | The winter of 1962–63, known as the Big Freeze of 1963, was one of the coldest winters (defined as the months of December, January and February) on record in the United Kingdom. Temperatures plummeted and lakes and rivers began to freeze over.

In the Central England Temperature (CET) record extending back to 1659, only the winters of 1683–84 and 1739–40 were colder than 1962–63.

The winter of 1962–63 remains the coldest since at least 1895 in all meteorological districts of the United Kingdom except Scotland North, where the two winters of 1978–79 and 2009–10 were colder.

On the 29th and 30th December 1962 a blizzard swept across South West England and Wales. Snow drifted to more than 20 feet (6.1 m) deep in places, driven by gale force easterly winds, blocking roads and railways. The snow stranded villagers and brought down power lines

29th | The 1962 South African Grand Prix was held in East London and won by Graham Hill. The victory also clinched the 1962 World Drivers Championship for Hill.

30th | Tradair, a failing British airline with nine airplanes, was acquired by East Anglian Flying Services, which renamed itself Channel Airways.

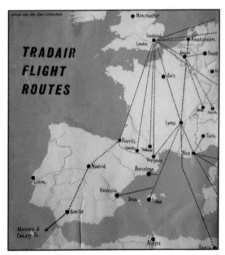 

A fireside chair on the race-course

A GRAND MODEL OF AN ABC TV TRANSMITTER VAN

DINKY SUPERTOYS No. 988—A.B.C. TV TRANSMITTER VAN

You've all enjoyed the "live" sporting spectacles on TV—horse racing, football, athletics, cricket, presented by the outside broadcasting units of B.B.C. and I.T.V. Here, now, is an excellent model of an O.B. (Outside Broadcasting) Transmitter Van in A.B.C. colours. It is fitted with a paraboloid plastic aerial which can be rotated through a complete circle and is detachable. Clear glazed windows in cab; white opaque material for the windows in the body. A companion vehicle shortly to be released is Dinky Supertoy No. 987 A.B.C. TV Mobile Control Room.

Length 4¾ in.   U.K. Price 7/9

DINKY SUPERTOYS

Published by MECCANO LTD., Binns Road, Liverpool 13, England   Printed by John Waddington Ltd., Leeds & London

The grey lag goose—winter visitor to Scotland's skies. Number 5 of a series, specially painted for Chivas Regal by C. F. Tunnicliffe R.A.

A COLD DAWN ... the gabble of the geese coming in; in line and echelon through the grey light. The flavour of such exciting moments is the flavour of Scotland--and so is the splendid taste of Chivas Regal Scotch Whisky. More than a century-and-a-half of tradition shapes the making of Chivas Regal—a skilful blend of Scotland's finest grain and malt whiskies, matured for 12 years before bottling.

Such a superb whisky costs more, naturally. Discerning people gladly pay more. For here you taste the glory of the Prince of Whiskies—that magnificent something extra that's the regal flavour of Scotland.

By appointment to
Her Majesty The Queen,
Purveyors of Provisions
and Scotch Whisky,
CHIVAS BROS. LTD.,
of Aberdeen.
Established since 1801.

SCOTLAND'S PRINCE OF WHISKIES

CHIVAS REGAL

12-YEARS-OLD *75° proof* **54/6**

MECCANO MAGAZINE

VOL. XLVII. No. 3   MARCH 1962   1/3

WUPPERTAL OVERHEAD RAILWAY

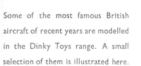

first name in motor caravans

When thoughts turn to motor caravans, it's the famous Dormobile that first comes to mind. And no wonder! It's the household word for modern living on wheels. So versatile, too. For taking John to the station, Paco and Peter to school, sundry Uncles and Aunts to the seaside, or the family on an extended tour, at home or abroad—a Dormobile's always ready for anything. (And think of what it can save on holiday hotel bills.) Only the genuine Dormobile has Martin Walter's vast coach-building experience behind it ... the unique 'Dormatic' convertible seating ... the distinctive elevating storm-proof roof with the wide-vision windows ..., and all the clever built-in fittings that put a genuine Dormobile out ahead, in a class of its own. Remember, it's a Martin Walter quality product.

Illustrated is the 6-seater 4-berth Dormobile caravan conversion of the Thames 10/12 or 15 cwt. van, from £816 10s. (no P.T.). 2-berth model from £741 10s. (no P.T.). Conversions of Bedford, Austin and Morris J4, Commer, Land-Rover and Volkswagen Vans also available.

STAND
88
MOTOR SHOW

– last word in versatility!

THE GENUINE **DORMOBILE** CARAVAN

Ask your dealer for a demonstration, or write for further details to the designers and builders.

DEPT. M
DORMOBILE WORKS
FOLKESTONE
Tel.: Folkestone 51844
Established 1773

Martin Walter Ltd

WORLD'S LARGEST PRODUCERS OF MOTORISED CARAVANS.

as THE MOTOR October 10 1962

JAGUAR

Grace... Space... Pace

SEE THE JAGUAR RANGE ON STAND 108 EARLS COURT

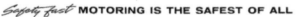

Safety Fast MOTORING IS THE SAFEST OF ALL

START WITH A MIDGET......

GRADUATE TO AN M.G.A.1600......

MARRY INTO A MAGNETTE........

MG MIDGET To own a Midget does something to you. It puts you in a class apart. Amongst the 'twin carburetter' men who revel in a good engine, in a car that sits the road and corners firm and true and steers and brakes with the M.G. safety touch. A car born of sporting success. A car for the enthusiast, built by enthusiasts with B.M.C. resources to supplement their skill. You start with the best in sports motoring when you buy a Midget. £472 plus £178.0.3 P.T.

M.G. MAGNETTE MARK IV Saloon
from £725 plus £272.17.9 P.T.
Automatic transmission optional £93.10.0 inc. P.T.

12 Months' Warranty and backed by B.M.C. Service—the most comprehensive in Europe.

The M.G. Car Co. Ltd. Sales Division, Cowley, Oxford. London Showrooms: Stratton Hse, 80 Piccadilly, W.1. Overseas Business: Nuffield Exports Ltd., Cowley, Oxford & 41 Piccadilly, W.1.

Family Motoring with Sporting Performance—

NEW
MAGNETTE
MK.IV

MORE POWER – EXTRA SAFETY

AUTOMATIC TRANSMISSION
(OPTIONAL)

WIDER TRACK – LONGER WHEEL BASE

On the road the less time you take overtaking—the greater your safety. M.G. sporting performance gives you that tremendous advantage. Those in the M.G. family, whether they drive the Midget, M.G.A. 1600, or the Magnette, are protected by having 'power-in-hand'—in addition, to all the other world-renowned M.G. 'Safety Fast' features. Think it over. The family motorist above all needs a Magnette—and what a joy it is to own one.

Safety Fast!

M.G. Midget £472 Plus £178.0.3. P.T.
M.G.A. 1600 Mk II open two-seater £663 Plus £303.2.3. P.T.
M.G. Magnette Mark IV Saloon £725 Plus £333.10.5.
All P.T. figures inclusive of surcharge.

THE M.G. CAR COMPANY LIMITED, COWLEY, OXFORD.   London Showrooms: Stratton Street, 80 Piccadilly, W.1   Overseas Business: Nuffield Exports Limited, Cowley, Oxford and 41 Piccadilly, W.1

A Queen all the world acknowledges

70° PROOF

HIGHLAND QUEEN

SCOTCH WHISKY

Macdonald & Muir Ltd

DISTILLERS LEITH SCOTLAND

MACDONALD & MUIR LTD

DISTILLERS

LEITH

SCOTLAND

Your Guarantee

Queen of Scots

APRIL 1962—119

Tops them all for fruitiness

ONLY ONE POINT

Assorted SPANGLES

Yours

Imagine the flavours of sweet, golden pineapples, big, ripe strawberries, refreshing limes—you'll find them all in every Spangles packet.

Each glistening sweet is neatly wrapped and the gay, red and yellow packet just naturally fits into your pocket or handbag.

What better value could you get for *one* point than Spangles . . . the wonderful new sweets with the rich fruity flavours!

SPANGLES

The new sweet treat by MARS

Flavours: STRAWBERRY · ORANGE · LEMON · BLACKCURRANT · LIME · PINEAPPLE

24

COST OF LIVING 1962

A conversion of pre-decimal to decimal money

ne Pound, 1971 became the year of decimalization when the pound became 100 new pennies. Prior to that
e pound was equivalent to 20 shillings. Money prior to 1971 was written £/s/d. (d being for pence). Below is
chart explaining the monetary value of each coin before and after 1971.

Symbol	Before 1971	After 1971
£	Pound (240 pennies)	Pound (100 new pennies)
s	Shilling (12 pennies)	5 pence
d	Penny	¼ of a penny
¼d	Farthing	1 penny
½d	Halfpenny	½ pence
3d	Threepence	About 1/80 of a pound
4d	Groat (four pennies)	
6d	Sixpence (Tanner)	2½ new pence
2s	Florin (2 shillings)	10 pence
2s/6d	Half a crown (2 shillings and 6 pence)	12½ pence
5s	Crown	25 pence
10s	10 shilling note (10 bob)	50 pence
10s/6d	½ Guinea	52½ pence
21s	1 Guinea	105 pence

Prices are in equivalent to new pence today and on average throughout the UK.

Item	1962	Price equivalent today
Wages, average yearly	£633.00	£12,729.00
Average house price	£2,552.00	£51,295.00
Price of an average car	£820.00	£16,482.00
Litre of petrol	£0.05p	£1.08p
Flour 1.5kg	£0.10p	£1.95p
Bread (loaf)	£0.05p	£1.09p
Sugar 1kg	£0.07p	£1.47p
Milk 1 pint	£0.14p	£2.81p
Butter 250g	£0.09p	£1.89p
Cheese 400g	£0.13p	£2.56p
Potatoes 2.5kg	£0.08p	£1.56p
Bacon 400g	£0.26p	£5.13p
Beer (Pint)	£0.09p	£1.68p

Life expectancy improves in United Kingdom

In 1962 the life expectancy in United Kingdom increased to 70.93 years.

This year, the life expectancy for women was 74 years and for men 68 years.
United Kingdom's position improved with respect to the 182 countries we publish life expectancy, dropping fro
13th in 1961 to 12th in 1962.

In Britain, Harold Macmillan was prime minister, presiding over a period of renewed prosperity following the
enforced frugality of the immediate post-war era. The annual inflation rate was 1.1%.

In other major news stories that year, screen legend Marilyn Monroe was discovered dead in the bedroom of h
Los Angeles home after an apparent overdose; Brazil retained the football World Cup, beating Czechoslovakia :
in the final in Chile and the first commercial communications satellite, Telstar, was successfully launched by the
US.

The top-selling single in the UK in 1962 was the yodelling Frank Ifield's I Remember You. Cliff Richard was the
golden boy of British pop, with The Young Ones and The Next Time/Bachelor Boy both topping the charts. The
teddy boy look was de rigueur among young males, with tight jeans all the rage for both sexes. Meanwhile, Lov
Me Do, the debut single by little-known Liverpool band the Beatles limped into the charts at number 17.

High-waisted trousers often exposed socks, and footwear consisted of polished Oxfords or chunky suede leathe
shoes called "creepers". Hairstyles included a greased back-and-up look with a quiff at the front and the side –
moulded to form something resembling a duck's behind from the men's hairstyling product, Brylcreem. Anothe
popular hairdo was the "Boston"; greased straight back and cut straight across the nape of the neck.

Where there are Teddy Boys there are also Teddy Girls. Their style also included tailored jackets and they coup
them with pencil skirts, (later, American poodle skirts) rolled-up jeans, and flat shoes or espadrilles. Finishing
touches could be straw boater hats or elegant clutch bags.

BRITISH BIRTHS

Eddie Izzard was born 7th February 1962 is an English stand-up comedian, actor, writer, and activist. Izzard began to toy with comedy at the University of Sheffield with student friend Rob Ballard. After leaving accountancy, Izzard and Ballard took their act to the streets. Izzard's big break came in 1991 after performing her "Raised by Wolves" sketch on the televised "Hysteria 3" AIDS benefit. She won a Primetime Emmy Award for Individual Performance in a Variety or Music Program for her 2000 comedy special Dress to Kill. In 1994, Izzard made her West End drama debut as the lead in the world premiere of David Mamet's The Cryptogram with Lindsay Duncan. She has appeared in numerous films, starting with 1996's The Secret Agent, and has appeared as several real-life individuals, including Charlie Chaplin in The Cat's Meow, actor Gustav von Wangenheim in Shadow of the Vampire, and General Erich Fellgiebel in Valkyrie. In 2009, she completed 43 marathons in 51 days for Sport Relief despite having no history of long-distance running. In 2016, she ran 27 marathons in 27 days in South Africa, raising £1.35 million.

eter Hugh Dennis was born the 13th February 1962 and is an English omedian, presenter, actor, writer, impressionist and voice-over artist, best nown for being one half of Punt and Dennis with comedy partner Steve unt. While an impressionist, Dennis did voices for Spitting Image and ppeared with Punt as resident support comics on two TV series hosted on he BBC by Jasper Carrott. Punt and Dennis' radio career includes over a ecade of performing Punt and Dennis, It's Been a Bad Week. In December 009, Dennis joined Oz Clarke in presenting the sixty minute Christmas pecial Oz and Hugh Drink to Christmas broadcast on BBC Two. In December 010 the pair returned for a four-part series called Oz and Hugh Raise the ar. Dennis has starred in a number of sitcoms, including My Hero, in which e played obnoxious GP Piers Crispin. From 2007 to 2014, he starred in utnumbered, a semi-improvised sitcom based around family life. In 2016 ennis appeared as the Bank Manager in the acclaimed BBC Three series eabag.

Vanessa Jane Feltz was born on the 21st February 1962 is an English television personality, broadcaster, and journalist. Vanessa Feltz was the first female columnist for The Jewish Chronicle and later joined the Daily Mirror. Feltz replaced Paula Yates on Channel 4's morning TV show The Big Breakfast, presenting a regular item where she interviewed celebrities whilst lying on a bed. She presented the ITV daytime television chat show, Vanessa, made by Anglia Television. She moved to the BBC to host a similar show, The Vanessa Show, in 1998 in a reported £2.7 million deal. In 2001, Feltz joined the local radio station BBC London 94.9 to present a mid-afternoon phone-in show. Also in 2001, Feltz was a contestant on the first series of Celebrity Big Brother. In 2010, Feltz and Ofoedu won their episode of the Virgin 1 show A Restaurant in our Living Room, preparing a dinner at their home for 25 people. On the 7th March 2011, Channel 5 moved The Vanessa Show to an afternoon slot at 14:15 following disappointing ratings for the morning slot.

Sir Steven Geoffrey Redgrave CBE DL was born on the 23rd March 1962 is a British retired rower who won gold medals at five consecutive Olympic Games from 1984 to 2000. Redgrave's primary discipline was sweep rowing, in which won Olympic Gold rowing both bowside and strokeside.

For much of his career he suffered illness: in 1992 he was diagnosed with ulcerative colitis and in 1997 he was diagnosed with diabetes mellitus type 2. Redgrave won gold medals at five consecutive Olympic Games from 1984 to 2000, plus a bronze medal at the 1988 Summer Olympics. Immediately after winning the 1996 Olympic Gold Medal, he stated that if anyone found him close to a rowing boat again, they could shoot him. However, he changed his mind shortly afterward, and resumed training after a four-month break. In 2000, he won his fifth consecutive Olympic Gold Medal and retired from the sport. In August 2000, prior to his final Olympic Games, the BBC broadcast Gold Fever, three-part BBC documentary which had followed the coxless fours in the years leading up to the Olympics.

Phillip Bryan Schofield was born on the 1st April 1962and is an English television presenter who works for ITV... After many years of writing letters to the BBC, at 17, Schofield took up the position of bookings clerk and tea boy for BBC Radio at Broadcasting House in London, where he was, at the time, the youngest employee. In the early 1990s, Schofield moved to adult-orientated television with various programmes for ITV, such as Schofield's Quest, Schofield's TV Gold and Ten Ball. From 1994 to 1997. Since 2002, Schofield has been a presenter on the ITV daytime show This Morning replacing John Leslie with Fern Britton until 2009 and with Holly Willoughby who replaced Britton in September that year. In May 2008. Since April 2008, he and Fern Britton hosted a revival of the ITV game show Mr. and Mrs., renamed as All Star Mr & Mrs. In 2010; the show took a break but returned in 2012 without Britton.

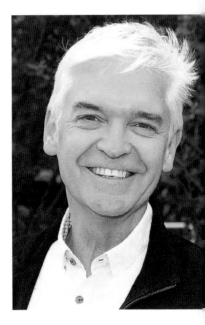

On 7 February 2020, Schofield came out as gay via a statement posted on his Instagram story, followed up in an interview on This Morning.

John David Hannah was born on the 23rd April 1962 is a Scottish film and television actor. After graduation, Hannah had parts in theatre productions, films and television, which included leading roles. He broke into the "big-time with his appearance as Matthew in Four Weddings and a Funeral (1994). On the 24th December 1997, Hannah and Scottish Films producer Murray Fergus established a production company called Clerkenwell Films. Clerkenwell's first big production was the Rebus series, including Black And Blue and The Hanging Garden. However, Rebus was later taken in-house by STV Productions, and Hannah was replaced in the leading role in the series by Ken Stott. He played the part of Quintus Lentulus Batiatus, the owner of a gladiator training house in Spartacus: Blood and Sand and the prequel Spartacus: Gods of the Arena. Hannah played the recurring role of scientist Holden Radcliffe on Agents of S.H.I.E.L.D. in a recurring role during season three and gets promoted to series regular during season four. Hannah married actress Joanna Roth on the 20th January 1996. The pair met several years before during a studio production.

James Warren "Jimmy" White, MBE was born on the 2ⁿᵈ May 1962 and is an English senior snooker player who has won 3 seniors World titles, and is the reigning champion. Nicknamed "The Whirlwind" because of his fluid, attacking style of play and popularly referred to as the "People's Champion". The World Championship has provided the theatre for White's greatest disappointments. In 1982, he led Alex Higgins 15–14 in their semi-final, was up 59–0 in the penultimate frame and was a red and colour away from the final. After missing a red with the rest, however, he could only watch as Higgins compiled a frame-winning 69 break. Higgins won the deciding frame that followed to reach the final. In 1984 White won the Masters, beating Terry Griffiths 9–5 in the final. In 1986 White reached his second Masters final, but was defeated by Cliff Thorburn. However, he won the Classic and also retained the Irish Masters title he won in 1985. Winning the World Seniors Championship in August 2019, White qualified for the 2019 Champion of Champions tournament where he narrowly lost 3–4 to Ronnie O'Sullivan in the first round.

⬝illip Christopher Jupitus was born 25ᵗʰ June 1962 and is an English stand-up ⬝d improv comedian, actor, performance poet, cartoonist and podcaster. ⬝⬝itus worked in Essex at the Manpower Services Commission, part of the ⬝partment of Employment, for five years, while he also wrote political poetry ⬝d drew cartoons. He resigned from the department in 1984, hoping for a ⬝reer in the music industry. His first vinyl recordings were part of the live ⬝wtown Neurotics album Kick-starting a Backfiring Nation as Porky the Poet in ⬝87. Jupitus toured colleges, universities and student unions, supporting bands ⬝ch as Billy Bragg, the Style Council and The Housemartins. In 2000, he released ⬝e stand-up comedy DVD Phil Jupitus Live: Quadrophobia. In 2001, he appeared ⬝ a sports journalist in the film Mike Bassett: England Manager. In 2002, Phil ⬝⬝itus was a stand-in presenter on BBC Radio 2 for Steve Wright while he was ⬝ay on holiday. Jupitus has presented several editions of the popular Top Ten ⬝ries for Channel 4, while also joining another comedy panel game—It's Only ⬝'...but I Like It—as a team captain, alongside Jonathan Ross and Julian Clary.

Michael Ashley Ball, OBE was born on the 27ᵗʰ June 1962 and is an English actor, singer and broadcaster. Ball played Alex in Aspects of Love, both in London and New York, and Giorgio in the London production of Stephen Sondheim's Passion. In September 2005, Ball made his New York City Opera debut as Reginald Bunthorne in Gilbert and Sullivan's Patience. Ball represented the UK in the Eurovision Song Contest 1992 held in Malmö, Sweden, singing the song "One Step Out of Time", which finished second. He has recorded 3 albums with Alfie Boe..... 2 reached number 1, Ball & Boe Together: in 2016, Ball & Boe: Together Again in 2017.

In April 2020, Ball recorded a duet with 99 year old World War II veteran Captain Tom Moore, in aid of the NHS during the COVID-19 pandemic. Their cover of "You'll Never Walk Alone" reached number one in the UK Singles Chart on the 24ᵗʰ April, not only giving Ball his first chart-topping single at the age of 57, but also making Moore the oldest ever person in history to score a number one hit.

Neil Anthony Morrissey was born on the 4th July 1962 and is an English actor, voice actor, comedian, singer and businessman. Neil Morrissey shot to fame the mid-1980s as dim biker Rocky in the ITV drama series Boon. In 1990, he played the lead role of Noddy in the British spoof horror film I Bought a Vam Motorcycle, which involved many of the actors from Boon. His role as Tony i Men Behaving Badly was created to replace the character of Dermot after H Enfield's departure from the series. The series became one of the most popu UK sitcoms of the 1990s and turned Morrissey into a national star and a targe for the tabloid newspapers. In 2002, Morrissey returned to TV screens in the drama series Paradise Heights which ran for two series. He then had a starrir role in the BBC sitcom Carrie and Barry from 2004 until 2005. In 2016, he joir the cast of Grantchester for the second series. He played the role of Harding Redmond. In 2017, he played the role of Greg McConnell in ITV's The Good Karma Hospital, and was Peter Carr in Series 3 of Unforgotten in 2018. He is supporter of Crystal Palace FC.

James Andrew Innes Dee was born on the 24th September 1961 and is an English stand-up comedian, actor, presenter and writer known for his sarcasm, irony and deadpan humour. Dee's first public act was an open-mic gig in 1986 at The Comedy Store, which he went to one evening after work. After he scooped the British Comedy Award for Best Stage Newcomer in 1991, Dee was offered his own show; The Jack Dee Show first went out on Channel 4 in February 1992, bringing him to a wider audience. His combination of stand-up routines on television continued with Jack Dee's Saturday Night on ITV, Jack Dee's Happy Hour in 1997 and later Jack Dee Live at the Apollo in 2004 on BBC One. In 2001, he won Celebrity Big Brother (then linked to fundraising for Comic Relief). During evictions, he dressed up in a tweed jacket and cap and held his packed suitcase, hoping to be voted out. In 2017 Dee co-wrote and starred in Bad Move, a sitcom about a middle-aged man and his wife who move from the city to a country cottage in search of the rural dream, which becomes more of a nightmare.

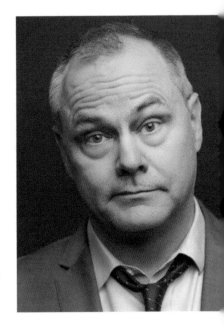

Alistair Murdoch McCoist, MBE was born on the 24th September 1962 is a Scottish former footballer who has since worked as a manager and pundit. McCoist began his playing career with Scottish club St Johnstone before moving to English side Sunderland in 1981. He returned to Scotland two yea later and signed with Rangers. McCoist had a highly successful spell with Rangers, becoming the club's record goal scorer and winning nine successiv league championships between 1988–89 and 1996–97. He later played for Kilmarnock. McCoist was inducted into the Scottish Sports Hall of Fame in 2007. He is also a member of the Scotland Football Hall of Fame, having gained 61 international caps. Towards the end of his playing career, McCois started his media career. Between 1996 and 2007, he was a team captain in the BBC sports quiz A Question of Sport. He succeeded Walter Smith as Rangers manager in 2011, but the club then suffered from serious financial difficulties. In September 2015 McCoist and Rangers mutually agreed to terminate his contract.

Michael John Flanagan was born on the 7th October 1962 and is an English comedian. Flanagan became a professional comedian in 1997 after attending a comedy course at Jacksons Lane in 1996. In 2001 he performed in the Big Value Comedy Show at the Edinburgh Fringe as one of four headline acts and in 2003 co-headlined a show with Nina Conti. He performed his first full-length solo show, What Chance Change? In 2006 and in 2007 was nominated for Best Newcomer at the Edinburgh Comedy Awards. Flanagan was a regular performer on Out to Lunch on Radio 2 in 2008 and appeared on Michael McIntyre's Comedy Roadshow in 2009. In 2010 he presented a four-part series for Radio 4 entitled Micky Flanagan: What Chance Change? and performed on Live at the Apollo, Stand Up for the Week and the Royal Variety Performance. In 2012 he starred alongside Mark Watson and host Mark Dolan as a captain on the Channel 4 advertising-based comedy panel programme The Mad Bad Ad Show. Micky's sell-out tour (and DVD) 'An Another Fing...' was the biggest comedy event of 2017 playing to over 600,000 people across the UK and Ireland, breaking box office records up and down the country.

ck Hancock was born on the 25th October 1962 and is an English actor and evision presenter. Nick Hancock appeared in two episodes of Mr. Bean, first a thief who stole Mr. Bean's camera, and later as a ticket inspector on a train. early television credits also include Me, You and Him and The Mary hitehouse Experience. In 1998 Hancock also provided the narration for a six-rt BBC documentary Pleasure Beach, following the running of the Blackpool usement park. After passing on the host's duties for both Room 101 and ey Think It's All Over, Hancock took a sabbatical to spend more time with his mily. He has made one-off appearances, including on Red Nose Day's The timate Makeover, in which Hancock, Anna Ryder Richardson, Phil Tufnell and gardener Joe Swift transformed a Liverpool play centre for children whose rents could not afford child-care. In 2009 he became the host of a daytime okery competition series, Taste the Nation, on ITV1. In 2011 he was asked by C America to join the panel of the NPR quiz show Wait Wait... Don't Tell Me! r a year-end special, "A Royal Pain in the News". Hancock won the game.

Jacqueline Jill Smith was born on the 3rd November 1962 is a British broadcaster, political commentator and former Labour politician. Having failed to be elected as a Labour MP for the safe Conservative seat of Mid Worcestershire in 1992, despite achieving a 4.9% swing, Smith was selected through an all-women shortlist in the 1997 general election as the Labour candidate for Redditch. Smith entered the Government in July 1999, as a Parliamentary Under-Secretary of State at the Department for Education and Employment, working with the Minister for School Standards Estelle Morris. She then became a Minister of State at the Department of Health following the 2001 general election. She was appointed as the Government's deputy Minister for Women in 2003, working alongside Secretary of State Patricia Hewitt. In this role she published the Government's proposals for Civil Partnerships, a system designed to offer same-sex couples an opportunity to gain legal recognition for their relationship with an associated set of rights and responsibilities.

BRITISH DEATHS

Stuart Fergusson Victor Sutcliffe born 23rd June 1940 and sadly passed away on the 10th April 1962. Known as Stu Sutcliffe he was a Scottish painter and musician better known as the original bass guitarist of the English rock band the Beatles. Sutcliffe left the band to pursue his career as a painter, having previously attended the Liverpool College of Art. Sutcliffe and John Lennon ar credited with inventing the name "Beetles", as they both liked Buddy Holly's band, the Crickets. John then came up with "The Beatles", from the word bea As a member of the group when it was a five-piece band, Sutcliffe is one of several people sometimes referred to as the "Fifth Beatle". In February 1962, he collapsed in the middle of an art class after complaining of head pains. German doctors performed tests, but were unable to determine the exact cause of his headaches. After collapsing again on 10th April 1962, he was take to the hospital, but died in the ambulance on the way there. The cause of death was later found to have been a brain haemorrhage – severe bleeding ir the right ventricle of his brain.

Sir Frederick Handley Page, CBE, FRAeS was born on the 15th November 1885 and died on the 21st April 1962. He was an English industrialist who was a pioneer in the aircraft industry and became known as the father of the heavy bomber. His company Handley Page Limited was best known for its large aircraft such as the Handley Page 0/400 and Halifax bombers and the H.P.42 airliner. The latter was the flagship of the Imperial Airways fleet between the wars and remarkable at the time for having been involved in no passenger deaths. He is also known for his invention, with Gustav Lachmann, of the leading edge slot to improve the stall characteristics of aircraft wings. Frederick Handley Page was the uncle of World War II flying ace Geoffrey Page. He died on the 21st April 1962 in Grosvenor Square, Westminster, London at age 76. The house in Grosvenor Square where Handley Page lived, No. 18, now bears a blue plaque. In 1987, Handley-Page was inducted into the International Air & Space Hall of Fame at the San Diego Air & Space Museum.

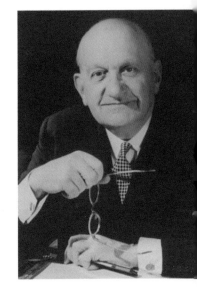

Robert MacGregor McIntyre was born on the 28th November 1928 and died on the 15th August 1962. He was a Scottish motorcycle racer. The first rider to achieve an average speed of 100 mph (160 km/h) for one lap of the Snaefell Mountain Course in 1957, McIntyre is also remembered for his five motorcycle Grand Prix wins which included three wins at the Isle of Man TT races, and four victories in the North West 200. The 1957 World Championship looked to be within reach, but a crash at Assen, in the Dutch TT meant he was out of action fc a couple of months. He did come second in the 500 cc Ulster Grand Prix, and wo the 350 cc Nations Grand Prix at Monza. His teammate Libero Liberati won the 500 cc World Championship that year, with McIntyre coming second. McIntyre was third in the 350 cc World Championship as well. In 1962 McIntyre finished second in the Spanish and French Grands Prix, while he had a non-start in the 50 Senior TT and mechanical problems in both the 250 and 350 cc events. He went on to win the Belgium GP at the Spa-Francorchamps circuit in the Ardennes, his last victory on the World stage.

SPORTING EVENTS 1962

1962 County Cricket Season

2 was the 63rd season of County Championship
cket in England. It was the last season to feature the
herable Gentlemen v Players fixture as a result of the
tinction between amateurs ("Gentlemen") and
ofessionals ("Players") being abolished following the
d of the season. As a result, all first-class cricketers
came nominally professional. Yorkshire won the
unty Championship. Yorkshire is the most successful
m in English cricketing history with 33 County
ampionship titles, including one shared. The team's
st recent Championship title was in 2015, following
from that achieved in 2014. Yorkshire plays most of
ir home games at the Headingley Cricket Ground in
ds. Another significant venue is at North Marine
ad Ground, Scarborough, which houses the annual
rborough Festival.

County Championship table

Team	Pld	Won	Lost	Drawn	No Decision	1st Inns Loss	1st Inns Draw	Bonus	Points	Average
Yorkshire	32	14	4	14	0	1	9	36	224	7.00
Worcestershire	32	14	3	14	1	1	8	34	220	6.87
Warwickshire	32	12	5	15	0	2	11	32	202	6.31
Gloucestershire	28	11	11	6	0	5	4	24	174	6.21
Surrey	28	10	3	14	1	2	9	32	174	6.21
Somerset	32	12	7	13	0	1	7	30	190	5.93
Derbyshire	28	8	6	13	1	2	8	28	144	5.14
Northamptonshire	28	7	5	16	0	1	10	22	128	4.57
Essex	28	8	6	13	1	2	7	12	126	4.50
Hampshire	32	7	5	19	1	2	11	30	140	4.37
Kent	28	7	9	10	2	2	3	16	110	3.92
Sussex	32	7	12	13	0	4	6	18	122	3.81
Middlesex	28	6	8	13	1	2	4	18	102	3.64
Glamorgan	32	6	13	13	0	1	4	14	96	3.00
Nottinghamshire	28	4	12	11	1	0	1	4	54	1.92
Lancashire	32	2	16	14	0	6	5	14	60	1.87
Leicestershire	28	2	12	13	1	2	5	12	50	1.78

1961–62 in English football

Ipswich Town Football Club is a professional association football club based in Ipswich, Suffolk, England. They play in League One, the third tier of the English football league system. The club was founded in 1878 but did not turn professional until 1936, and was subsequently elected to join the Football League in 1938. They play their home games at Portman Road in Ipswich. The only fully professional football club in Suffolk, they have a long-standing and fierce rivalry with Norwich City in Norfolk, with whom they have contested the East Anglian derby 148 times since 1902. The club's traditional home colours are blue shirts with white shorts and blue socks.

Ipswich have won the English league title once, in their first season in the top flight in 1961–62, and have twice finished runners-up, in 1980–81 and 1981–82. They won the FA Cup in 1977–78, and the UEFA Cup in 1980–81. They have competed in all three major European club competitions, and have never lost at home in European competition, defeating Real Madrid, A.C. Milan, Inter Milan, Lazio and Barcelona, among others.

Pos	Team	Pld	HW	HD	HL	AW	AD	AL	AGF	AGA	Pts
1	Ipswich Town	42	17	2	2	7	6	8	35	39	56
2	Burnley	42	14	4	3	7	7	7	44	41	53
3	Tottenham Hotspur	42	14	4	3	7	6	8	29	35	52
4	Everton	42	17	2	2	3	9	9	24	33	51
5	Sheffield United	42	13	5	3	6	4	11	24	46	47
6	Sheffield Wednesday	42	14	4	3	6	2	13	25	35	46
7	Aston Villa	42	13	5	3	5	3	13	20	36	44
8	West Ham United	42	11	6	4	6	4	11	27	45	44
9	West Bromwich Albion	42	10	7	4	5	6	10	33	44	43
10	Arsenal	42	9	6	6	7	5	9	32	41	43
11	Bolton Wanderers	42	11	7	3	5	3	13	27	44	42
12	Manchester City	42	11	3	7	6	4	11	32	43	41
13	Blackpool	42	10	4	7	5	7	9	29	45	41
14	Leicester City	42	12	2	7	5	4	12	34	44	40
15	Manchester United	42	10	3	8	5	6	10	28	44	39
16	Blackburn Rovers	42	10	6	5	4	5	12	17	36	39
17	Birmingham City	42	9	6	6	5	4	12	28	46	38
18	Wolverhampton Wanderers	42	8	7	6	5	3	13	35	52	36
19	Nottingham Forest	42	12	4	5	1	6	14	24	56	36
20	Fulham	42	8	3	10	5	4	12	28	40	33
21	Cardiff City	42	6	9	6	3	5	13	20	48	32
22	Chelsea	42	7	7	7	2	3	16	29	65	28

1961–62 Scottish Division One

1961–62 Scottish Division One was won by Dundee by ~~ee~~ points over nearest rival Rangers. It is the only Scottish ~~gue~~ title win in Dundee's history. St Johnstone and Stirling ~~ion~~ finished 17th and 18th respectively and were relegated ~~he~~ 1962-63 Second Division. St Johnstone was relegated on ~~average~~, with the teams in 15th, 16th and 17th all ~~shing~~ on 25 points.

~~ndee~~ F.C. was formed in 1893 by the merger of two local ~~s~~, East End and Our Boys, with the intention of gaining ~~tion~~ to the Scottish Football League (SFL). Their application ~~successful~~ and they played their first League game on 12 ~~ust~~ 1893 at West Craigie Park, securing a 3–3 draw against ~~gers~~. Dundee struggled during the first 10 years of their ~~stence~~. Their best league position was fifth which they ~~ieved~~ in seasons 1895–96 and 1896–97. They also reached ~~semi-finals~~ of the Scottish Cup in 1894–95 and 1897–98, ~~ng~~ to Renton and Kilmarnock respectively.

Pos	Team	Pld	W	D	L	GF	GA	GR	Pts
1	Dundee (C)	34	25	4	5	80	46	1.739	54
2	Rangers	34	22	7	5	84	31	2.710	51
3	Celtic	34	19	8	7	81	37	2.189	46
4	Dunfermline Athletic	34	19	5	10	77	46	1.674	43
5	Kilmarnock	34	16	10	8	74	58	1.276	42
6	Hearts	34	16	6	12	55	49	1.122	38
7	Partick Thistle	34	16	3	15	60	55	1.091	35
8	Hibernian	34	14	5	15	58	72	0.806	33
9	Motherwell	34	13	6	15	65	62	1.048	32
10	Dundee United	34	13	6	15	70	71	0.986	32
11	Third Lanark	34	13	5	16	59	60	0.983	31
12	Aberdeen	34	10	9	15	60	73	0.822	29
13	Raith Rovers	34	10	7	17	51	73	0.699	27
14	Falkirk	34	11	4	19	45	68	0.662	26
15	Airdrieonians	34	9	7	18	57	78	0.731	25
16	St Mirren	34	10	5	19	52	80	0.650	25
17	St Johnstone (R)	34	9	7	18	35	61	0.574	25
18	Stirling Albion (R)	34	6	6	22	34	76	0.447	18

1962 Five Nations Championship

The 1962 Five Nations Championship was the thirty-third series of the rugby union Five Nations Championship. Including the previous incarnations as the Home Nations and Five Nations, this was the sixty-eighth series of the northern hemisphere rugby union championship. Ten matches were played between 13th January and 17th November. It was contested by England, France, Ireland, Scotland and Wales.

A smallpox epidemic in South Wales in March and April caused the match between Ireland and Wales to be postponed until November 1962.

France became champions for the third time.

Table

Position	Nation	Games				Points			Table points
		Played	Won	Drawn	Lost	For	Against	Difference	
1	France	4	3	0	1	35	6	+29	6
2	Scotland	4	2	1	1	34	23	+11	5
3	England	4	1	2	1	19	16	+3	4
3	Wales	4	1	2	1	9	11	−2	4
5	Ireland	4	0	1	3	9	50	−41	1

Results

Scotland	3–11	France
England	0–0	Wales
Wales	3–8	Scotland
England	16–0	Ireland
France	13–0	England
Ireland	6–20	Scotland
Scotland	3–3	England
Wales	3–0	France
France	11–0	Ireland
Ireland	3–3	Wales

The Masters 1962

e 1962 Masters Tournament was the 26th Masters Tournament, held
ril 5–9 at Augusta National Golf Club in Augusta, Georgia. Arnold Palmer
n the third of his four Masters titles in the tournament's first three-way
yoff. It was the fifth of his seven major titles. The other two in the 18-
le Monday playoff were also major championship winners: defending
ampion Gary Player and Dow Finsterwald, winner of the PGA
ampionship in 1958. Out in 37 and down three strokes to Player at the
n, Palmer shot a 31 on the back nine for 68, while Player shot a 71 and
sterwald a 77. In the lead after three rounds, Palmer was five-over for
final round after a double bogey at the 10th hole. After five pars, he
died 16 and 17 to get into the Monday playoff with a 75 (+3). The gallery
the playoff was estimated at 16,000 spectators.

nry Picard, the 1938 champion, made his final cut at Augusta at age 55. Jack Nicklaus, 22, tied for 15th in his
urth appearance, the first as a professional. He won the next major, the U.S. Open, in a playoff over Palmer at
kmont near Pittsburgh. With near misses in 1959 and 1961, Palmer said that it could have been his fifth
nsecutive title at Augusta.

e 36-hole cut was increased this year to include the low 44 plus ties and anyone within 10 shots of the lead
eviously it was the low 40 plus ties). 110 players entered the tournament and 52 made the cut at 149 (+5).

uce Crampton won the third Par 3 contest with a score of 22.

Place	Player	Country	Score	To par	Money ($)
T1	Arnold Palmer	United States	70-66-69-75=280	−8	Playoff
	Gary Player	South Africa	67-71-71-71=280		
	Dow Finsterwald	United States	74-68-65-73=280		
4	Gene Littler	United States	71-68-71-72=282	−6	6,000
T5	Jerry Barber	United States	72-72-69-74=287	−1	3,600
	Jimmy Demaret	United States	73-73-71-70=287		
	Billy Maxwell	United States	71-73-72-71=287		
	Mike Souchak	United States	70-72-74-71=287		
T9	Charles Coe (a)	United States	72-74-71-71=288	E	0
	Ken Venturi	United States	75-70-71-72=288		2,000

Place	Player	Country	Score	To par	Money ($)
1	**Arnold Palmer**	United States	68	−4	20,000
2	Gary Player	South Africa	71	−1	12,000
3	Dow Finsterwald	United States	77	+5	8,000

Grand National 1962

The 1962 Grand National was the 116th renewal of the Grand National horse race that took place at Aintree Racecourse near Liverpool, England, on 31 March 1962.

The race was won by Kilmore, a 28/1 shot ridden by jockey Fred Winter. The 12-year-old horse was trained by Ryan Price. Wyndburgh was second, and Mr. What finished third. Thirty-two horses ran and all returned safely to the stables.

The BBC covered its third Grand National with David Coleman again at the helm on Grand National Grandstand. Peter O'Sullevan, Bob Haynes and Peter Montague-Evans provided the commentary.

Triple Crown Winners 1962

2,000 Guineas

Privy Councillor was a British Thoroughbred racehorse and sire, best known for winning the classic 2000 Guineas in 1962. After winning three minor races as a two-year-old he went on to win the Free Handicap in the spring of 1962 before recording an upset win in the Guineas. He never won again and made little impact as a breeding stallion. Privy Councillor was a chestnut horse, bred by his owner Gerald Glover at his Pytchley House stud in Northamptonshire. He was sired by Counsel, the winner of the 1955 Greenham Stakes and two edition of the Rose of York Stakes. Privy Councillor's dam High Number was bought by Glover as a foal for 750 guineas and showed modest ability on the track, winning two minor races as a four-year-old.

St Leger

Hethersett was a British Thoroughbred racehorse and sire best known for falling when favourite for The Derby and then winning the classic St Leger Stakes in 1962. After showing promise as a two-year-old he was the highest rated British three-year-old of 1962 when he also won the Brighton Derby Trial and the Great Voltigeur Stakes. After his success in the Leger, when he gave his trainer Dick Hern his first classic win, Hethersett never won again and was retired in 1963. He had a brief but successful stud career before his death at the age of seven.

The Derby

Larkspur was an Irish Thoroughbred racehorse and sire who won the Derby in 1962. He was the first of six Derby winners trained by Vincent O'Brien at Ballydoyle. Larkspur achieved little of note either before or after his Epsom triumph. Larkspur, a light chestnut horse with a white blaze, was bred in Ireland by Philip Love. His sire, the American-bred Derby winner Never Say Die, was a qualified success at stud, getting the double Classic winner Never Too Late and becoming Champion Sire in 1962, largely thanks to Larkspur's earnings. Apart from Larkspur his dam Skylarking produced eight winners, the best being the 1965 Dante Stakes winner Ballymarais. Ballymarais ran in the 2000 Guineas and was nearest at finish at 33-1, and when the weights for the Dante were published he carried only 7.11 and was 1-4 on for the race, which he duly won, he was trained by Bill Gray, owned by Bill Stoker and ridden by Brian Connorton.

1962 British Grand Prix

he 1962 British Grand Prix was a Formula One motor race held at Aintree on 21 July 1962. It was ace 5 of 9 in both the 1962 World Championship f Drivers and the 1962 International Cup for ormula One Manufacturers. This was the last ace at Aintree. From 1963 onwards, the race ould be held at Silverstone.

cotsman Jim Clark dominated the race, driving a otus 25. It was considered a power track enefitting the light and powerful Lotus and Lola ars in particular. Ferrari were still side-lined due o the Italian metal workers' strike but managed o send one car for Phil Hill.

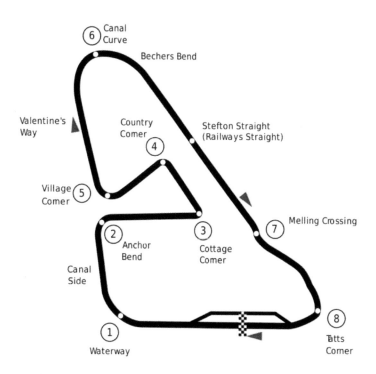

Final Placings

Pos	No	Driver	Constructor	Laps	Time/Retired	Grid	Points
1	20	Jim Clark	Lotus-Climax	75	2:26:20.8	1	9
2	24	John Surtees	Lola-Climax	75	+ 49.2	2	6
3	16	Bruce McLaren	Cooper-Climax	75	+ 1:44.8	4	4
4	12	Graham Hill	BRM	75	+ 1:56.8	5	3
5	30	Jack Brabham	Lotus-Climax	74	+ 1 Lap	9	2
6	18	Tony Maggs	Cooper-Climax	74	+ 1 Lap	13	1
7	34	Masten Gregory	Lotus-Climax	74	+ 1 Lap	14	
8	22	Trevor Taylor	Lotus-Climax	74	+ 1 Lap	10	
9	8	Dan Gurney	Porsche	73	+ 2 Laps	6	
10	42	Jackie Lewis	Cooper-Climax	72	+ 3 Laps	15	

was not a particularly exciting race, with Clark leading from start to finish and fairly large gaps between the rs. Out of the twenty-one starters, six still had four-cylinder engines while the rest were multi-cylinder cars. ese cars were in a sort of class of their own, with Jackie Lewis finishing best of the four-cylinder cars. John rtees' Lola started and finished in second place, in spite of having lost second gear on the tenth lap. Dan urney was hopeful after winning in France and at the non-championship Solitude race in the preceding two eeks. He began the race in third but had a slipping clutch and slid steadily down the field, ending in ninth osition. His teammate Jo Bonnier had to retire with a broken transmission. Bruce McLaren (Cooper) passed urney after twelve laps and finished in third. Graham Hill pushed his BRM hard but had to settle for fourth, and as threatened by Jack Brabham in the closing stages.

1962 Wimbledon Championships

The 1962 Wimbledon Championships took place on the outdoor grass courts at the All England Lawn Tennis and Croquet Club in Wimbledon, London, United Kingdom. The tournament was held from Monday 25th June until Saturday 7th July 1962. It was the 76th staging of the Wimbledon Championships, and the third Grand Slam tennis event of 1962. Rod Laver and Karen Susman won the singles titles.

Men's Singles

Rod Laver successfully defended his title, defeating Martin Mulligan in the final, 6–2, 6–2, 6–1 to win the Gentlemen's Singles tennis title at the 1962 Wimbledon Championships.

Women's Singles

Karen Susman defeated Věra Suková in the final, 6–4, 6–4 to win the Ladies' Singles tennis title at the 1962 Wimbledon Championships. Angela Mortimer was the defending champion, but lost in the fourth round to Suková.

Men's Doubles

Roy Emerson and Neale Fraser were the defending champions, but lost in the semi-finals to Boro Jovanović and Nikola Pilić.

Bob Hewitt and Fred Stolle defeated Jovanović and Pilić in the final, 6–2, 5–7, 6–2, 6–4 to win the Gentlemen' Doubles tennis title at the 1962 Wimbledon Championship.

Women's Doubles

Billie Jean Moffitt and Karen Susman successfully defended their title, defeating Sandra Price and Renée Schuurman in the final, 5–7, 6–3, 7–5 to win the Ladies' Doubles tennis title at the 1962 Wimbledon Championships.

Mixed Doubles

Fred Stolle and Lesley Turner were the defending champions, but lost in the semi-finals to Neale Fraser and Margaret DuPont.

Fraser and DuPont defeated Dennis Ralston and Ann Haydon in the final, 11–9, 6–2 to win the Mixed Doubles tennis title at the 1962 Wimbledon Championships.

Rod Laver

Karen Susman

BOOKS PUBLISHED IN 1962

[C]lockwork Orange is a dystopian satirical black comedy novel by [En]glish writer Anthony Burgess, published in 1962. It is set in a near-[fut]ure society that has a youth subculture of extreme violence.

[Th]e teenage protagonist, Alex, narrates his violent exploits and his [exp]eriences with state authorities' intent on reforming him. The [boo]k is partially written in a Russian-influenced argot called [Na]dsat", which takes its name from the Russian suffix that is [equ]ivalent to '-teen' in English. According to Burgess, it was a jeu [d'e]sprit written in just three weeks.

[In 2]005, A Clockwork Orange was included on Time magazine's list of [the] 100 best English-language novels written since 1923, and it was [nam]ed by Modern Library and its readers as one of the 100 best [Eng]lish-language novels of the 20th century. The original manuscript [of t]he book has been kept at McMaster University's William Ready [Div]ision of Archives and Research Collections in Hamilton, Ontario, [Can]ada since the institution purchased the documents in 1971. It is [con]sidered one of the most influential dystopian books.

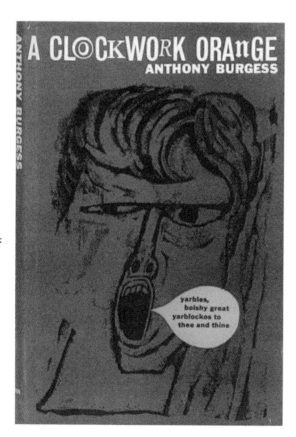

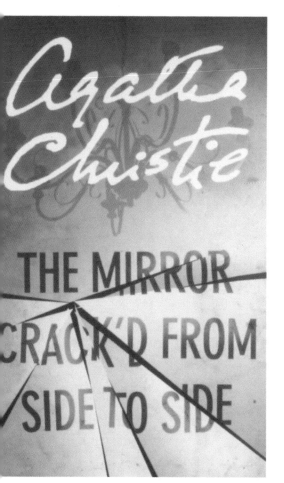

The Mirror Crack'd from Side to Side is a work of detective fiction by Agatha Christie and first published in the UK by the Collins Crime Club on the 12th November 1962 and in the US by Dodd, Mead and Company in September 1963 under the shorter title of The Mirror Crack'd and with a copyright date of 1962. The UK edition retailed at fifteen shillings (15/-) and the US edition at $3.75.

It is set in the fictional English village of St. Mary Mead and features Miss Marple. It was dedicated by Christie: "To Margaret Rutherford, in admiration."

The novel received good reviews on publication, for "the shrewd exposition of what makes a female film star tick", and being easy to read, though the plot was not as "taut" as some of Christie's novels. A later review found it "one of the best of her later books" and liked the way that "the changes in village life and class structure since the war are detailed".

The title of the novel comes from the poem The Lady of Shalott by Alfred, Lord Tennyson. The Lady of Shalott lives in a tower near Camelot, and sees it only reflected in a glass. She will be doomed if she looks directly; when Lancelot appears, she looks directly at him and Camelot and the looking glass cracks.

The IPCRESS File is Len Deighton's first spy novel, published in 1962. The story involves Cold War brainwashing, includes scenes in Lebanon and on an atoll for a United States atomic weapon test, as well as information about Joe One, the Soviet Union's first atomic bomb. The story was made into a film in 1965 produced by Harry Saltzman, directed by Sidney J. Furie and starring Michael Caine.

In 1992 Deighton said that the inspiration to write the novel came from his real-life neighbour Anna Wolkoff, a White Russian émigré who collaborated with a cipher clerk from the American embassy to spy for Germany in World War II. Deighton's mother cooked for Wolkoff's dinner parties and he said that he "vividly" remembered when British MI5 agents came to arrest her: "The experience was a major factor in my decision to write a spy story at my first attempt at fiction." The plot involves mind control, the acronym IPCRESS of the title standing for "Induction of Psycho-neuroses by Conditioned Reflex under Stress". The brainwashing is similar to a shock technique called psychic driving pioneered by Donald Ewen Cameron in the 1950s, originally on unwitting mental hospital patients, which was used and funded by the Central Intelligence Agency's secret MKULTRA program in Canada.

LEN DEIGHTON
The master of fictional espionage

The Ipcress File

'Changed the shape of the espionage thriller'
DAILY TELEGRAPH

The Spy Who Loved Me is the ninth novel (and tenth book) Ian Fleming's James Bond series, first published by Jonathan Cape on the 16th April 1962. It is the shortest and most sexu explicit of Fleming's novels, as well as a clear departure from previous Bond novels in that the story is told in the first pers by a young Canadian woman, Vivienne Michel. Bond himself does not appear until two-thirds of the way through the boc Fleming wrote a prologue to the novel giving Michel credit a co-author.

Due to the reactions by critics and fans, Fleming was not hap with the book and attempted to suppress elements of it whe he could: he blocked a paperback edition in the United Kingdom and only gave permission for the title to be used when he sold the film rights to Harry Saltzman and Albert R. Broccoli, rather than any aspects of the plots. However, the character of Jaws is loosely based on one of the characters in the book and a British paperback edition was published afte his death. A heavily adapted version of The Spy Who Loved M appeared in the Daily Express newspaper in daily comic strip format in 1967–1968. In 1977 the title was used for the tent film in the Eon Productions series. It was the third to star Ro Moore as Bond and used no plot elements from the novel.

land is the final book by English writer Aldous Huxley, published 1962. It is the account of Will Farnaby, a cynical journalist who shipwrecked on the fictional island of Pala. Island is Huxley's opian counterpart to his most famous work, the 1932 dystopian vel Brave New World. The ideas that would become Island can seen in a foreword he wrote in 1946 to a new edition of Brave w World:

nglishman William Asquith "Will" Farnaby deliberately wrecks his at on the shores of the Kingdom of Pala, an island halfway tween Sumatra and the Andaman Islands, thus forcing his entry this otherwise "forbidden island". Farnaby, a journalist, political uckster, and lackey for the oil baron Lord Joseph "Joe" Aldehyde, tasked with persuading the island's current queen—the Rani— sell Aldehyde rights to Pala's untapped oil assets. Farnaby vakens on the island with a leg injury, hearing a myna bird reaming "Attention", when a local boy and girl notice him and ke him for medical treatment to their grandfather, Dr. Robert acPhail. Dr. Robert and a young man named Murugan ailendra carry Farnaby to Robert's house for a surprisingly iccessful hypnotherapy session led by Susila, Robert's daughter--law and the mother of the two children

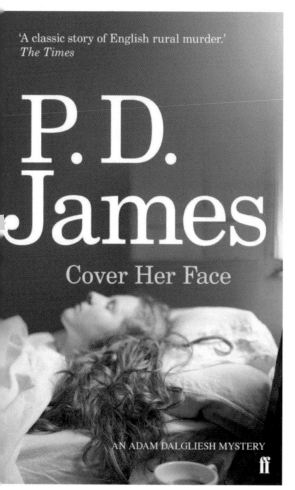

Cover Her Face. The story opens with a dinner party hosted by Mrs. Eleanor Maxie at Martingale, a medieval manor house in the (fictional) Essex village of Chadfleet. Mrs. Maxie's son and daughter, Stephen Maxie and Deborah Riscoe, are both at the party. Serving at the party is Sally Jupp, an unmarried mother with an infant son, who was employed by Mrs. Maxie.

Deborah later goes to London and visits Stephen at the hospital where he works and sees her brother talking with Sally. Stephen says that Sally brought him some of their terminally ill father's tablets, which she found on old Mr. Maxie's bed. Stephen suspects that Mr. Maxie manages to deceive his devoted servant Martha, pretending to take his tablets when he is simply hiding them in his bed. On the day of St. Cedd's church fete, Sally announces that Stephen has asked her to marry him. The following day, Martha complains that Sally has overslept again. On entering the room, Sally's lifeless body is found. Detective Chief Inspector Adam Dalgliesh and Detective Sergeant Martin arrive and begin their investigation. It emerges that Sally had been secretly married to James Ritchie, who has a successful job in Venezuela, but he returns to England after her death. Sally had blackmailed her uncle (who unbeknownst to her had spent her modest trust fund) into giving her 30 pounds.

Lolita. James Mason plays professor Humbert Humbert, who while waiting to begin a teaching post in the United States rents a room from blowzy Shelley Winters. Winters immediately falls for the worldly Humbert, but he only has eyes for his landlady's nubile daughter Lolita. The professor goes so far as to marry Winters so that he can remain near to the object of his ardour. Turning up like bad penny at every opportunity is smarmy TV writer Quilty (Peter Sellers), who seems inordinately interested in Humbert's behaviour When Winters happens to read Humbert's diary, she is so revolted by his lustful thoughts that she runs blindly into the street, where she is struck and killed by a car. Without telling Lolita that her mother is dead, Humbert packs her into the car and goes on a cross country trip, dogged every inch of the way by a mysterious pursuer. Once she gets over the shock of her mother's death, Lolita is agreeable to inaugurating an affair with her stepfather (this is handled very, very discreetly, despite the slavering critical assessments of 1962).

Budget $2,000,000

Run time is 2h 33mins

Trivia
Peter Sellers modelled the voice of his character Clare Quilty on that of his director, Stanley Kubrick.

Sue Lyon did not attend the New York premiere in June '62, as she was too young to see the film. However, she was allowed to attend the London premiere at the Columbia Theatre, in September.

Stanley Kubrick originally wanted Joey Heatherton for the title role of Lolita, but Heatherton's father Ray Heatherton said no - for fear his daughter would be typecast as a promiscuous sex kitten.

The Humbert Humbert role was originally offered to Cary Grant, who turned it down in indignation.

Goofs
When Humbert is considering shooting Charlotte while she supposedly is taking a bath, he uncorks and drinks from a liquor bottle, tossing the cork onto the end table. Seconds later he is shown with the same cork in his left hand, which he then places on the end table.

Director Stanley Kubrick walks out of the very first interior shot (centre to right bottom) of Humbert entering Quilty's house.

There is a moving shadow of a crew member on Humbert's back when he is talking to Lolita in the kitchen of her house; the same movements can be seen in a crew member's reflection on the television screen facing the camera.

When Humbert urges Mrs. Richard T. Schiller to leave her husband and return to him, the shadow of the boom mic is visible on the back wall.

Lawrence of Arabia. A semi-fictional account of the exploits of British military officer T.E. Lawrence during WWI is presented, plus a prologue at his 1935 funeral where his contemporaries remark or don't remark at how they consider him and his military contributions especially to the Great War. Viewed somewhat as an insolent man, he, a lieutenant in intelligence at a desk job in the Cairo bureau, is assigned to go on a reconnaissance mission to the Arabian peninsula to assess Prince Faisal's efforts against the Turks. He is assigned this job in what is considered its low importance in the British still focusing their own efforts directly on the German offensive, and because of his academic knowledge of Arabia. Against the narrow confines of his original orders and advice of ranking officers in the field, Lawrence, befriending many he meets, not only the Prince but most specifically Sherif Ali, bands with the Arabs in being able to coalesce the many disparate tribes which comprise the fighting Bedouins.

Box office Cumulative Worldwide Gross: $45,715,757

Run time 3h 48mins

via

s movie was banned in many Arab countries as they felt Arab historical figures and the Arab peoples were srepresented. Omar Sharif arranged a viewing with President Gamal Abdel Nasser of Egypt to show him that ere was nothing wrong with the way they were portrayed. Nasser loved the movie and allowed it to be eased in Egypt, where it went on to become a monster hit.

his first location scouting trip in Jordan, director Sir David Lean discovered the remains of the Turkish omotives and railroad tracks T.E. Lawrence had destroyed during the Arab Revolution. After forty years in the ι, they hadn't even rusted.

Alec Guinness was made up to resemble the real Faisal as closely as possible. When they were shooting in ·dan, several people who knew the man mistook him for the real thing.

ɔofs

e airplanes used during the raid were DH Tiger Moths. They did not go into production until late 1929-early 30.

the attack on Aqaba, a white pickup truck can be seen in the background parked next to some white buildings.

ring the attack on Aqaba, a Turkish soldier is seen with a Browning M1919 machine gun. Which would not have en in use at the time of the Arabian revolt (1917) and it would not have been used by the Turks.

the opening scenes set in 1935, not only are three phase electricity cables visible in many shots, but a colour HF television transmitter is also visible over Lawrence's right shoulder.

THE RARE FILM STORY OF A FATHER WHO MUST EXPOSE HIS CHILDREN TO A SMALL TOWN'S OUTRAGED PASSIONS...AND CAN ONLY PROTECT THEM WITH HIS LOVE.

PULITZER PRIZE WINNER GREATEST BEST SELLER OF THE DECADE!

GREGORY PECK

TO KILL A Mockingbird

NOT SUITABLE FOR CHILDREN

with MARY BADHAM as 'Scout' · PHILLIP ALFORD as 'Jem' · JOHN MEGNA
RUTH WHITE · PAUL FIX · BROCK PETERS · FRANK OVERTON
Screenplay by HORTON FOOTE · Based upon Harper Lee's novel "To Kill a Mockingbird"
Music by ELMER BERNSTEIN · Directed by ROBERT MULLIGAN · Produced by ALAN PAKULA
A Pakula-Mulligan, Brentwood Productions Picture · A UNIVERSAL RELEASE

To Kill A Mockingbird. It carries us on an odyssey through the fire of prejudice and injustice in 1932 Alabama. Presenting her tale fir as a sweetly lulling reminiscence of events from her childhood, th narrator draws us near with stories of daring neighbourhood exploits by her, her brother "Jem," and their friend "Dill." Peopled with a cast of eccentrics, Maycomb, a "tired and sleepy town" modelled after Lee's native Monroeville, finds itself as the venue the trial of Tom Robinson, a young black man falsely accused of raping an ignorant white woman. Atticus Finch, Scout and Jem's widowed father and deeply principled man, is appointed to defen Tom for whom a guilty verdict from an all-white jury is a foregone conclusion. Juxtaposed against the story of the trial, is the childre hit and run relationship with Boo Radley, a shut-in whom the children, and Dill's Aunt Rachel, suspect of insanity, and whom no one has seen in recent history.

Winner of 3 Oscars.	Best Actor in a Leading Role	Gregory P
	Best Writing, Screenplay	Horton Fo
	Best Art Direction	

Run time 2h 09mins.

Trivia

Mary Badham (Scout) and Gregory Peck (Atticus) became close during filming, and kept in contact for the rest of his life. Peck always called her "Scout", her character role, while Badham called Peck "Atticus".

Brock Peters (Tom Robinson) started to cry while filming his testifying scenes, without rehearsing it this way and Gregory Peck (Atticus Finch) said that he looked past him, instead of looking at him in the eye, to avoid choking up himself.

After being offered the role of Atticus Finch, Gregory Peck quickly read Harper Lee's novel in one sitting and called director Robert Mulligan immediately afterwards to say that he would gladly play it.

The watch used in the film was a prop, but Harper Lee gave Gregory Peck her father's watch after the film was completed, because he reminded her so much of him.

Goofs

At the beginning of the film a penny in the cigar box dated 1960 are shown in the lower right corner of the screen, while the story is set in the year 1932.

The "melon" Crayola crayon shown in the opening sequence was not introduced until 1949. The film is set in 1932.

With the story set in 1932, the "ham" costume Mary Badham (Scout) wore was clearly made from fiberglass, not papier mache. Fiberglass was invented in 1932-1933 by Russell Games Slayter of Owens-Corning, as a material to be used as thermal building insulation. The first commercial production of glass fibre was in 1936. I seriously doubt that anyone in Maycomb, Alabama would have had access to fiberglass at that time.

Dr. No. James Bond 007, seductive British Secret Agent, has been sent to Jamaica to investigate the disappearance of British Agent John Strangway and his secretary. Once arriving, 007 become suspicious of scientist Professor Dent, who was the last person to have seen Strangway before he disappeared. After learning Professor Dent is working for a terrorist with a metal hand, Dr. Julius No, and Strangway is dead, 007 meets C.I.A. Agent Felix Leiter and his assistant Quarrel in Jamaica. 007 and Quarrel head to the tropical island Crab Key, after encountering the beautiful Honey Ryder, 007 finds the island is Dr. No's secret lair, and 007 and Honey are captured, but Quarrel is killed. Where 007 learn Dr. No is has been disrupting the American rocket launches at N.A.S.A., and he is out for world domination and plots to unleash his vengeance on the United States of America. Can James Bond defeat Dr. No and save the world?

Box Office
Budget:$1,100,000 (estimated)
Gross USA: $16,067,035
Cumulative Worldwide Gross: $16,079,357

Run time 1h 50mins

ivia

of the sets and furniture were slightly smaller than they would be in reality, so that Bond would look larger.

ntrary to popular belief, Sir Sean Connery was not wearing a hairpiece in his first two outings as James Bond. hough he was already balding by the time Dr. No was in production, he still had a decent amount of hair and e filmmakers used varying techniques to make the most of what was left. By the time of Goldfinger (1964), nnery's hair was too thin and so various toupees were used for his last Bond outings.

is was chosen to be the inaugural movie in the James Bond film franchise as the plot of the source novel was e most straightforward. It had only one major location (Jamaica) and only one big special effects set piece.

lores Keator was given the role of Strangways' secretary because she owned the house in which the crew ere shooting.

oofs

hen a bunch of birds suddenly take off in the jungle, the sound effects are of monkeys screaming, instead of rds chattering or wings flapping.

e shadow of a boom mic is visible on the hotel room wall behind Bond, just after the room service attendant nds him his martini.

the river, the breathing tubes are supposedly cut from the very thin reeds growing on the bank, but after ey're cut, they're clearly much thicker bamboo stalks.

The Man Who Shot Liberty Valance. When Senator Ransom Stoddard returns home to Shinbone for the funeral of Tom Doniphon, he recounts to a local newspaper editor the story behind it all. He had come to town many years before, a lawyer by profession. The stage was robbed on its way in by the local ruffian, Liberty Valance, and Stoddard has nothing to his name left save a few law books. He gets a job in the kitchen at the Ericson's restaurant and there meets his future wife, Hallie. The territory is vying for Statehood and Stoddard is selected as a representative over Valance, who continues terrorizing the town. When he destroys the local newspaper office and attacks the editor, Stoddard calls him out, though the conclusion is not quite as straightforward as legend would have it.

Nominated for 1 Oscar. Another 4 wins & 2 nominations.

Box Office
Budget:$3,200,000 (estimated)

Run time 2h 03mins

Trivia

Several reasons have been put forward for the film being in black and white. John Ford once claimed it added to the tension, but others involved with the production said Paramount was cutting costs, which was why the film was shot on sound stages at the studio. Without the budget restraints, Ford would have been in Monument Valley using Technicolor stock.

Woody Strode frequently performed his own stunts, partly because he was such a good athlete and partly because it was hard to find a black double to match his build and looks (this had also been the case on Spartacus (1960)). In the scene where Doniphon sets fire to his house, Strode had to race in and drag him out of the building. John Wayne was using a double but the 47-year-old Strode wasn't. John Ford told his star, "Duke, Woody is an old man, and he's got to carry you and he doesn't need a double!" Wayne decided to do the scene without one.

Goofs

One of the songs being played in the saloon was "Hot Time In The Old Town Tonight," but the song was written in 1896 by Theodore Metz, several years after the time the story is set in.

On the train ride home one can see a modern diesel freight train riding on the tracks in the background. Then the same exact footage is run again.

In the gunfight between Stoddard and Valance, Valance's hat falls off and lands in the dirt. During the flashback scene, the hat lands on the boardwalk.

In the reverse shot during the climactic political rally, the opposing parties switch sides.

Bette Davis and Joan Crawford

Sister, sister,

oh so fair,

why is there blood

all over your hair?

"WHAT EVER HAPPENED TO BABY JANE?"

What Ever Happened To Baby Jane? In 1917, Baby Jane is a famous, but spoiled child star that performs a show with her father under the jealous look of her sister Blanche. In 1935, Blanche Hudson becomes a famous and glamorous actress in Hollywood and the untalented Baby Jane Hudson only acts because Blanche forces the producers to give parts to her. One night, they go to a party and there is a car accident. In 1962, Blanche is a crippled woman that has been left wheelchair-bound after the accident that lives with her alcoholic sister Baby Jane in a decaying Hollywood mansion. Baby Jane does not recall the accident since she was drunk and is in absolute control over Blanche that is completely isolated without any contact with the outside world and dumping her correspondence in the trash. As Baby Jane becomes more insane, she decides to return to the stage and hires the idle Edwin Flagg to play piano. Meanwhile she continues to torment Blanche and her cruelty increases.

Won 1 Oscar. Another 3 wins & 11 nominations.

Box Office
Budget:$980,000 (estimated)

Run time 1h 45mins

ia

te Davis had a Coca-Cola machine installed on set. This was to deliberately provoke Joan Crawford, who the widow of Pepsi chairman Alfred Steele, and a celebrity spokesperson for the company.

te Davis and Joan Crawford worked hard to promote the film, both knowing that their profit percentage its would pay off in spades with the film's success. Davis travelled to 17 theatres across the state of New k in three days for personal appearances and helped give away promotional "Baby Jane" dolls to patrons a "lucky envelope" under his or her seat.

film was a smash hit upon initial release, recouping its original budget in only 11 days, and eventually ssing $9 million. In adjusted 2017 dollars, this would be equivalent to $72,596,920.53.

ulah Bankhead, Claudette Colbert, Olivia de Havilland and Marlene Dietrich were considered to play nche.

ofs

nche screws up the note to throw it to her neighbour. However, when Jane hands the folded note to nche it has no sign of having been screwed up. Apart from folded, the paper is pristine.

en Jane is preparing to dump Elvira's body and is interrupted by her female neighbour who has just driven in the dark, it is clear before the cut that the person who actually drives the car onto the driveway was a le stage hand.

n the end of the movie Baby Jane's mole does not appear on her cheek.

How the West Was Won. Sprawling epic which follows the Prescott's, an emigrant family through four generations, from the Erie Canal in the 1830's to their settled home in the West a half a century later. On the way they encounter river pirates, and escape with the help of fur trapper Linus Rawlings, who subsequently marries one of their daughters, Eve. The parents are drowned on a foundering raft, and the other daughter Lilith becomes a riverboat singer and catches the eye of a genteel adventurer Cleve Van Valen. They cross the plains together in a wagon train and make and lose a fortune in California; meanwhile Linus has turned farmer and, comes the Civil War, joins the Union Army and is killed at the Battle of Shiloh. One of his sons Zeb also joins the army and stays after the war as a cavalry officer and is sent to Colorado to help guard the pioneering railroad against the Indians, whose land they are crossing. By this time Lilith is the elderly lady of the family, having survived long enough to see the dream of settlement realized, but not, mercifully, the aerial shots of the Los Angeles freeway traffic with which the film ends.

Won 3 Oscars. Another 7 wins & 5 nominations.

Run time 2h 44mins

Trivia

Due to the detail that would have been shown via the Cinerama process, the costumes had to be sewn by hand, rather than with a sewing machine, as they would have been during the time periods depicted in the movie.

Although James Stewart's character was only supposed to be 28 in the movie, Stewart was actually 53 at the time of filming.

Spencer Tracy was only able to narrate the film rather than play a part due to his health problems.

Gary Cooper had been offered the role of Linus Rawlings but died before filming began. James Stewart then accepted the part despite feeling miscast.

During filming in June 1961, Karl Malden had to be rushed to hospital to have an emergency appendectomy.

Goofs

In the train portion, when Zeb Rawlings is alerted to riders ahead, and climbs on the coal tender, they show the tracks in front. To the left you can see a twin set of high tension power poles.

Ma and Pa Prescott are buried on the bank of the river in which they drowned. When Eve visits her parent's grave decades later, there is no sign of a river anywhere near the farm.

When Linus Rawlings throws a dagger into the chest of one of the bandits, the wire guiding it can be seen against the tent.

At the very end of the movie, when the camera flies under the Golden Gate bridge, it and its operator can be seen reflected in the windshield of the (presumably) helicopter used for filming.

If you come in five minutes after this picture begins, you won't know what it's all about! when you've seen it all, you'll swear there's never been anything like it!

Frank Sinatra
Laurence Harvey
Janet Leigh

The Manchurian Candidate

Angela Lansbury Henry Silva James Gregory
GEORGE AXELROD...JOHN FRANKENHEIMER ...... JOHN FRANKENHEIMER
GEORGE AXELROD .... RICHARD CONDON ......HOWARD W KOCH

The Manchurian Candidate. Major Bennett Marco (Frank Sinatra) is an intelligence officer in the U.S. Army. He served valiantly as a Captain in the Korean war and his Sergeant, Raymond Shaw (Laurence Harvey), even received the Medal of Honour. Marco has a major problem however: he has a recurring nightmare, one where two members of his squad were killed by Shaw. He's put on indefinite sick leave and visits Shaw in New York City. Shaw, for his part. has established himself well, despite the misgivings of his domineering mother, Mrs. Eleanor Shaw Iselin (Dame Angela Lansbury). She is a red-baiter, accusing anyone who disagrees with her right-wing reactionary views of being a Communist. Raymond hates her, not only for how she's treated him, but equally because of his stepfather, the ineffectual U.S. Senator John Iselin (James Gregory), who is intent on seeking higher office. When Marco learns that others in his Korean War unit have had nightmares similar to his own, he realizes that something happened to all of them in Korea, and that Raymond Shaw is the focal point.

Nominated for 2 Oscars. Another 5 wins & 6 nominations.

Run time 2h 06mins

·ivia

·ank Sinatra broke the little finger of his right hand on the desk in the fight sequence with Henry Silva. Due to ·-going filming commitments, he could not rest or bandage his hand properly, causing the injury to heal correctly. It caused him chronic discomfort for the rest of his life.

·cording to Executive Producer Howard W. Koch, the budget was two million two hundred thousand dollars. Of ·at amount, one million dollars went for Frank Sinatra's salary, with another two hundred thousand dollars for ·urence Harvey, leaving only one million dollars for everything else.

· his own admission, Frank Sinatra's best work always came in the first take. Writer, Producer, and Director John ·ankenheimer always liked the idea of using the freshness of a first take - so nearly all of the key scenes ·aturing Sinatra are first takes, unless a technical problem prevented them from being used.

oofs

· the opening sequence the bar in Korea has a US flag with 50 stars. During the Korean War there were only 48 ·ates and hence only 48 stars on the US Flag.

·e live TV cameras in the senate hearing and press conference carry the NBC logo used at the time the film was ·ade, not the logo used at the time the story takes place.

·hen Rosie picks up Ben at the police station, you can clearly see an actor in the background with no pants on ·ying to sneak out of the scene.

·e camera's shadow is visible on the bust of Abraham Lincoln.

The Longest Day. England in June 1944. Unseasonal storms. Allied troops are massed ready for the invasion of France, some already on the boats. The Normandy beaches will be their destination while paratroopers are dropped inland to take key towns and bridges. On the other side of the Channel the Germans still expect the invasion at Calais, and anyway the weather makes them think nothing is likely to be imminent. Eisenhower decides to go. Hitler sleeps on.

Academy Awards, USA 1963

Oscar Winners	**Best Cinematography, Black-and-White**
	Jean Bourgoin, Walter Wottitz
	Best Effects, Special Effects
	R.A. MacDonald (visual)
	Jacques Maumont (audible)
Oscar Nominee	**Best Picture**
	Best Art Direction-Set Decoration
	Best Film Editing

Run time 2h 58mins

Trivia

Henry Grace was not an actor when being cast as Dwight D. Eisenhower, but his remarkable resemblance to Eisenhower got him the role.

While clearing a section of the Normandy beach near Ponte du Hoc, the crew unearthed a tank that had been buried in the sand since the original invasion. Mechanics cleaned it off, fixed it up and it was used in the movie as part of the British tank regiment.

An estimated 23,000 troops were supplied by the US, Britain and France for filming (Germans only appeared as officers in speaking roles). The French contributed 1000 commandos, despite their involvement in the Algerian War at the time.

Dwight D. Eisenhower walked out on the movie after only a few minutes, frustrated by the inaccuracies.

Goofs

Gen. Gavin is wearing a Senior Parachutist badge in 1944.The Parachutist Badge was formally approved on 10 March 1941. The senior and master parachutist's badges were authorized by Headquarters, Department of the Army, in 1949 and were announced by Change 4, Army Regulation 600-70, dated 24 January 1950.

When the ships are about to begin bombarding the beaches you see a group of planes fly by the camera. These are Douglas Sky Raiders, which did not see service until the late 1940s.

When the French first attack the casino there is barbed wire, but when they run from the hotel to the casino there is none.

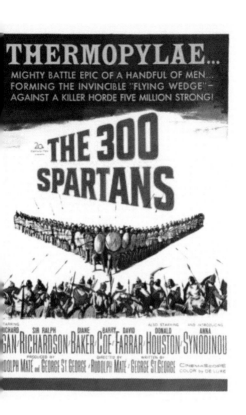

The 300 Spartans. The Persian king of kings Xerxes has devoted his reign to realizing the ambition of his father, stopped by Greeks, to extend his Achaemenid slave empire to and beyond Greece, and marches in 480 BC with an unprecedentedly vast army. When a captured Spartan explorer shows unconditional courage even on the chopping block, he is spared and sends to the assembled Greek states at Corinth to report the Persian might. There the Athenian leader Themistocles manages to turn the defeatist tide by formally placing the Athenian fleet under the supreme command of Sparta, whose king Leonidas promises to defend Greece regardless who follows- but back in Sparta, the ruling council hesitates to commit the whole army until the Persians approach the Corinthian Isthmus, and even after an encouraging Delphi oracle -loose a king or all Sparta- is forbidden to lead it before the end of a religious festival, so he takes off first, keeping his promise, with only his 300 mean strong bodyguard.

Run time 1h 54mins

Trivia

This film was released in 1962, a time when there was a world-wide craze for sword and sandal epics set in the ancient Greco-Roman world that were being produced in Italy and often involving heroes with super-human strength.

Though shooting commenced in Greece in November 1960 and the film was completed and copyright dated 1961, Fox seemed to be in no hurry to get it to the cinemas. After the Philadelphia premiere in August 1962, it was submitted to the British Board of Film Censors on 10th September 1962 and passed with a "U" certificate. The London premiere finally arrived on 25th October 1962 when it ran at the Rialto for a quite respectable five weeks. The UK general release at normal prices was from 11th November 1962.

At the time, this movie was considered the most violent movie in America.

Goofs

While most of the Spartans wear the correct headgear, Leonidas and his officers wear Roman legionnaire style helmets that wouldn't be around for about 200 years.

Rigid stirrups are shown in use by horse riders; however, this type of stirrup wasn't in use until some centuries later. The first dependable representation of paired stirrups dates to around 322 A.D.

When the Persian army is into Greece where they will meet the Spartans, they are marching between mountains on their left, and water on their right. In actuality, the Persians were marching south along the eastern edge of Greece, so the water would have been on their left with mountains on their right. The way the movie portrays it, the Persians are marching out of Greece.

During the battle with the immortals, one of the Spartan "officers" is revealed to have a pink towel between his forearm and the shield itself to comfort and protect the forearm. This is revealed a couple of times during the battles.

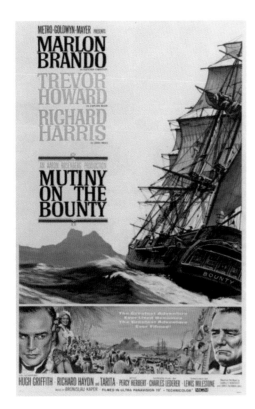

Mutiny On The Bounty. In 1787, in Portsmouth, the rude Captain William Bligh of the British ship Bounty is assigned to travel to Tahiti to transplant breadfruit to bring to England. Bligh is jealous of the aristocratic 1st Lt. Fletcher Christian and along the journey, his tyrannical and cruel behaviour leads to a showdown with the rebel Seaman John Mills and other seamen. But on the voyage of returning to England, his savage attitudes kill crewmembers, forcing Fletcher to lead a mutiny to overthrow Bligh. What will be the consequences of this action?

Oscar nominee for:

Best Picture
Best Cinematography, Colour
Best Art Direction-Set Decoration, Colour
Best Film Editing
Best Effects, Special Effects
Best Music, Original Song
Best Music, Score - Substantially Original

Run time 3h 05mins

Trivia

Marlon Brando, wearing his naval uniform, was widely booed and jeered at the New York City premiere, while Trevor Howard received thunderous applause. Brando walked out of the cinema after the audience started laughing at his English accent.

Marlon Brando's notorious on-set antics reached a pinnacle on this film. According to Peter Manso's Brando biography, Brando had so much clout by this point that he got MGM to green-light virtually every outrageous idea he had. At one point, he pulled people off the film crew to decorate and design a friend's wedding in Tahiti. Another time, he had airplanes filled with cases of champagne, turkeys and hams flown to Tahiti for parties.

Richard Harris had such a horrible time on the film that he refused to attend the premiere.

Goofs

Francis Drake is reported as the man who brought potatoes to the Old World, but they were actually carried by the Spanish after the conquest of Peru.

When Bligh lands on the beach in Tahiti he orders the cutter in close. As he walks up the beach a sailor in the background from the cutter jumps out of the boat leans down and puts on a pair of sunglasses.

In the movie, Christian dies on the beach as the Bounty burns. In reality, there are no beaches on Pitcairn, and Christian died much later at the hands of the Tahitian men during subsequent conflicts on the island.

The actual mutiny did not happen in the manner portrayed in the film. Christian and the other mutineers actually took the ship in the early hours of the morning, while Bligh and almost everyone else were asleep.

It starts in Portsmouth Harbour on 23rd December yet trees in the background are in full leaf plus it is very sunny and looks warm, very unusual for England just before Christmas.

MUSIC 1962

Artist	Single	Reached number one	Weeks at number one
1962			
liff Richard and The Shadows	The Young Ones	11th January 1962	6
vis Presley	Can't Help Falling in Love	22nd February 1962	4
he Shadows	Wonderful Land	22nd March 1962	8
Bumble and the Stingers	Nut Rocker	17th May 1962	1
vis Presley	Good Luck Charm	24th May 1962	5
ike Sarne with Wendy Richard	Come Outside	28th June 1962	2
ay Charles	I Can't Stop Loving You	12th July 1962	2
rank Ifield	I Remember You	26th July 1962	7
lvis Presley	She's Not You	13th September 1962	3
he Tornados	Telstar	4th October 1962	5
rank Ifield	Lovesick Blues	8th November 1962	5
lvis Presley	Return To Sender	13th December 1962	3

62 and although rock & roll is still on a bit of a hiatus, beach music makes its debut. The Beach Boys sign a cording contract with Capital Records and release two singles, "Surfin Safari" and "409", their first single urfin'" which was originally released in 1961 finds a new audience and renewed chart success. Later that year ey would release an album, "Surfin' Safari". They were inspired to some degree by the unique guitar sounds of ck Dale and the Del-Tones. Dale's unorthodox use of reverberators and loud amplifiers sought to mimic the ensity of crashing ocean waves. Nicknamed "King of The Surf Guitar" his single "Misirlou" made it to the top of e chart. His concert events were called "surfer stomps" because of the stomping of their surf sandals while tening.

other first this year was a young performer who was making the rounds at the New York coffee houses named b Dylan. He had come to New York to visit his idol and later mentor Woody Guthrie. He was earning extra oney by playing harmonica as part of session for another folk singers album when he was asked to audition for own album. His first album which was self-titled "Bob Dylan" was a bit of a flop. The album had two original ngs on it, "Talkin' New York" and "Song to Woody" the rest was covers of other folk songs. Commercially popular it never reached the charts not even in later years but it did give a glimpse into the unique style and rytelling capacity of this great performer.

BILLBOARD 1962

Cliff Richard and The Shadows

"The Young Ones"

"**The Young Ones**" is a single by Cliff Richard and the Shadows. The song, written by Sid Tepper and Roy C. Bennett, is the title song to the 1961 film The Young Ones and its soundtrack album.

With advance orders of over 500,000, it was released in January 1962 on the Columbia (EMI) label and went straight to No. 1 in the UK Singles Chart, the first British single to do so. It held that position for six weeks and spent 20 weeks in the chart. It has sold 1.06 million copies in the UK, and 2.6m worldwide.

The track was included on Cliff Richard and the Shadows No. 1 EP Hits from the Young Ones.

In the 1980s, it became the theme song to the alternative comedy sitcom The Young Ones.

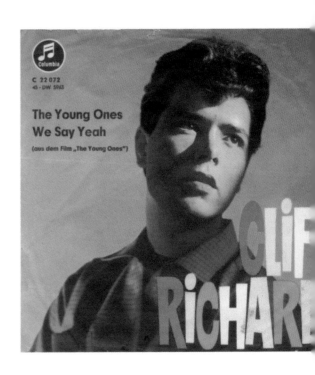

Elvis Presley

"Can't Help Falling In Love"

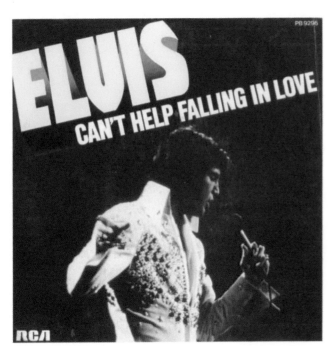

"**Can't Help Falling in Love**" is a song recorded by American singer Elvis Presley for the album Blue Hawaii (1961). It was written by Hugo Peretti, Luigi Creatore, and George David Weiss and published by Gladys Music, Inc. The melody is based on "Plaisir d'amour" a popular French love song composed in 1784 by Jean-Paul-Égide Martini. The song was initially written for a woman as "Can't Help Falling in Love with Him", which explains the first and third line ending on "in" and "sin" rather than words rhyming with "you".

"Can't Help Falling in Love" was featured in Presley's 1961 film Blue Hawaii. During the following four decades, it has been recorded by numerous other artists, including Bob Dylan on his 1973 album Dylan, Tom Smothers, Swedish pop group A-Teens, and the British reggae group UB40, whose 1993 version topped the U.S. and UK charts.

The Shadows

"Wonderful Land"

onderful Land" is an instrumental piece written by Jerry
dan recorded and released as a single by the Shadows in
52. It stayed at No. 1 for eight weeks in the UK Singles Chart.

dan had previously written the hugely successful "Apache"
the Shadows in 1960, and "Wonderful Land" was recorded
May 1961 by the Shadows' original line up of Hank Marvin,
ce Welch, Jet Harris and Tony Meehan. The strings were
ded later by producer Norrie Paramor.

the time of the song's release, Tony Meehan had left the
up to be replaced by Brian Bennett who co-wrote the B-side
ars Fell on Stockton". The group was in a period of transition
d whilst the song was at No. 1 Jet Harris left to be replaced by
an Locking.

B. Bumble and the Stingers

"Nut Rocker"

"Nut Rocker" is an instrumental rock single recorded by American instrumental ensemble B. Bumble and the Stingers that reached number 23 in the U.S. Billboard Hot 100 in March 1962 and went to number 1 in the UK Singles Chart in May 1962. It is a version of the march from Tchaikovsky's ballet The Nutcracker. The recording was made by the house band of session musicians at Rendezvous Records in Los Angeles, including drummer Earl Palmer and guitarist René Hall, who had already had hits in the US charts with rocked-up versions of "In the Mood". At the time of its original release in the UK, the BBC had a policy of banning records which parodied classical music. "Nut Rocker" was put to committee, which decided that "this instrumental piece is quite openly a parody of a Tchaikovsky dance tune, is clearly of an ephemeral nature, and in our opinion will not offend reasonable people", and was not therefore banned.

Elvis Presley

"Good Luck Charm"

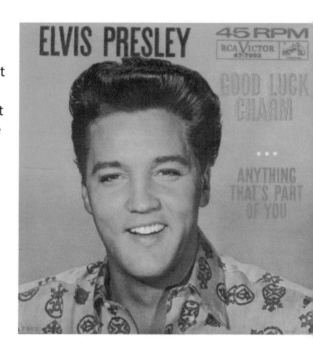

"**Good Luck Charm**" is a song recorded by Elvis Presley and published by Gladys Music, Elvis Presley's publishing company that reached number 1 on the Billboard Hot 100 list in the week ending 21st April 1962. It remained at the top of the list for two weeks. It was also no. 1 on the Cash Box chart in the U.S. It reached number 1 in the UK Singles Chart in the week ending 24th May 1962 and stayed there for five weeks.

The song was written by Aaron Schroeder and Wally Gold and recorded at RCA Studio B in Nashville, Tennessee by Presley on the 15th October 1961. It completed his second hat-trick of chart topping singles in the UK. Presley is joined vocally on the chorus by Jordanaires first tenor Gordon Stoker.

Mike Sarne with Wendy Richard

"Come Outside"

"**Come Outside**" was a number one in the UK Singles Chart in 1962 for Mike Sarne, and the actress Wendy Richard, who provided vocal interjections. The track stayed at No.1 for a fortnight during the weeks commencing 28th June and 5th July 1962. The song was placed twelfth on the chart of overall single sales for the calendar year 1962 in the UK. In 1991, Samantha Fox, Frank Bruno, Liz Kershaw and Brun Brookes recorded a cover version of the song as the officia Children in Need single of the year.

Mike Sarne was born Michael Scheuer at St Mary's Hospita Paddington, London. He is of Czechoslovakian descent. Active in the 1960s as singer he had three more releases which made the UK Singles chart: "Will I What?" in 1962, which featured Billie Davis; "Just for Kicks", in 1963; and "Code of Love", also in 1963.

Ray Charles

"I Can't Stop Loving You"

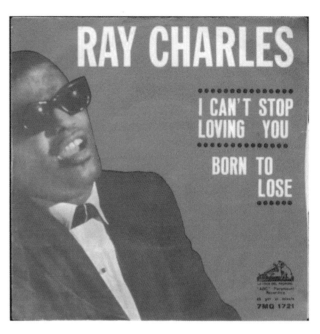

Can't Stop Loving You" is a popular song written and omposed by country singer, songwriter, and musician Don ibson.

he song was covered by Ray Charles in 1962, featured on harles' Modern Sounds in Country and Western Music, and eleased as a single. Charles' version reached number one on e Billboard Hot 100 in 1962, for five weeks. This version ent to number one on the U.S. R&B and Adult ontemporary charts. Billboard ranked it as the No. 2 song r 1962. Charles reached No. 1 in the UK Singles Chart in ly 1962, staying for two weeks.

he Ray Charles version is noted for his saying the words efore the last five lines of the song on the final chorus: "Sing e Song, Children".

Frank Ifield

"I Remember You"

"I Remember You" is a popular song, published in 1941. Australian singer Frank Ifield recorded the song in a yodelling country-music style on the 27th May 1962, and his version went to number one on the UK Singles Chart selling 1.1 million copies in the UK alone.

The recording stayed at No.1 for seven weeks. It also reached number five on the U.S. Billboard Hot 100 and number one on the U.S. Easy Listening chart.

Glen Campbell covered the song on his 1987 album Still Within the Sound of My Voice. His version peaked at number 32 on the Billboard Hot Country Singles chart in 1988.

Elvis Presley

"She's Not You"

"She's Not You" is a 1962 song recorded by Elvis Presley and released as a single.

"She's Not You" reached No. 5 on the Billboard Hot 100 and No. 13 on the R&B chart. In the UK, the single reached No. 1 where it stayed for three weeks. It was also the first song on the new Irish Charts to reach number one on the 5th October 1962.

The song was recorded on the 19th March 1962. It was published by Elvis Presley Music, Inc., Elvis Presley's publishing company.

The Jordanaires sang background vocals.

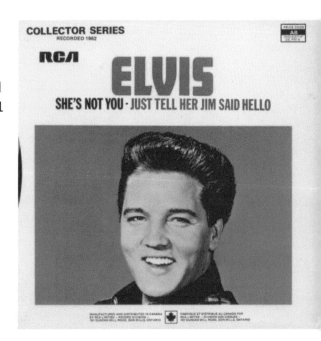

The Tornados

"Telstar"

"Telstar" is a 1962 instrumental written and produced by Joe Meek for the English band the Tornados. The track reached number 1 on the U.S. Billboard Hot 100 in December 1962 (the second British recording to reach number 1 on that chart in the year, after "Stranger on the Shore" in May), and was also a number one hit in the UK Singles Chart. It was the second instrumental single to hit number 1 in 1962 on both the US and UK weekly charts.

The record was named after the Telstar communications satellite, which was launched into orbit on the 10th July 1962. Written and produced by Joe Meek, it featured either a clavioline or the similar Jennings Univox, both keyboard instruments with distinctive electronic sounds. "Telstar" won an Ivor Novello Award and is estimated to have sold at least five million copies worldwide.

Frank Ifield

"Lovesick Blues"

ovesick Blues". In December 1962, Frank Ifield's version of ovesick Blues" topped the UK Singles Chart, and reached mber 44 on the Billboard Hot 100 the following month. amophone compared his singing to a "rough and raucous nmie Rodgers". Meanwhile, Elizabethan delivered a negative view, stating: "No true country singer would dare do to a nk Williams number what Frank Ifield has done to 'Lovesick ues'." The review finished by declaring that Ifield had "none Jim Reeves' depth and character, nor of the subtle melodic ality (of) Don Gibson." By the end of February 1963, lboard estimated that the single had sold close to a million pies worldwide.

e song first appeared in the 1922 musical Oh, Ernest. It was corded by Emmett Miller in 1925 and 1928, and later by untry music singer Rex Griffin.

Elvis Presley

"Return To Sender"

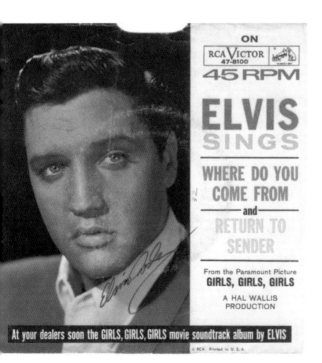

"Return to Sender" is a 1962 hit single recorded by American singer Elvis Presley and performed in the film Girls! Girls! Girls! The song was written by Winfield Scott and Otis Blackwell and published by Elvis Presley Music. The song peaked at number one on the UK Singles Chart and was the UK Christmas number one of 1962. It was also the first Christmas number one in the Irish Singles Chart. In the United States, "Return to Sender" reached #2 on the American Billboard singles chart, kept out of the top spot by The Four Seasons' "Big Girls Don't Cry.

"Return to Sender" came back in vogue in 1993 when the U.S. Postal Service issued a commemorative postage stamp honouring Presley on what would have been his 58th birthday. Fans mailed envelopes franked with first-day issues of this stamp to fictitious addresses so that they would receive their letters back, marked with the words "return to sender."

WORLD EVENTS 1962

January

1st | The Beatles auditioned unsuccessfully for Decca Records with John Lennon, Paul McCartney, George Harrison and, at that time, drummer Pete Best. The first song of 15 performed between 11:00 am and noon was "Like Dreamers Do". The audition tape was officially released in 1982. Decca opted instead to sign the other group that auditioned that day-- Brian Poole and the Tremeloes. Both groups would have hit recording of the song Twist and Shout, with the Tremeloes hitting #1 in the U.K. and the Beatles #4 in the U.S.

3rd | A spokesman for Pope John XXIII revealed that Cuban leader Fidel Castro and several other officials had received a decree of excommunication from the Roman Catholic Church in 1961 under two sections of canon law, for impeding bishops in their work and for violence against clergymen. In September, Cuban bishop Eduardo Boza Masvidal and 135 priests had been forced to leave Cuba.

5th | Prison inmate Clarence Gideon sent a letter, written in pencil, to the United States Supreme Court, asking them to reverse his conviction for burglary on the grounds that he had not been given the right to an attorney. The Supreme Court granted certiorari and, on the 18th March 1963, issued the landmark decision of Gideon v. Wainwright, holding that the Sixth Amendment guarantee, of the right to assistance of counsel, required the appointment of a lawyer for any person unable to afford one.

7th | A bomb exploded at the Paris apartment building where controversial existentialist author Jean-Paul Sartre lived. Sartre was not home at the time, and his mother was not injured, but the fire destroyed most of his unpublished manuscripts.

10th | An avalanche on Mount Huascarán, the tallest peak in Peru killed 4,000 people. At 6:13 pm, melting ice triggered the slide of three million tons of ice, mud and rock down the side of Huascaran, quadrupled in size as it gathered mass, and, within eight minutes, buried the town of Ranrahirca (population 2,700) the village of Yanamachico, and three other villages totalling 800 residents. Ranrahirca, which had only 50 survivors, would be rebuilt, and then destroyed again in an earthquake and an even larger avalanche on the 31st May 1970.

11th | Soviet submarine B-37, nine days away from being dispatched to Cuba, was moored at Polyarny, conducting maintenance and pressurizing of outdated gas-steam torpedoes. At 8:20 am, a fire in the torpedo compartment detonated all twelve torpedoes and instantly destroying the submarine. Captain Anatoly Begeba, who had been outside, inspecting the top of the sub, survived. The 78 men inside the sub drowned as it sank to the bottom of the Barents Sea.

15th | After the United Kingdom sought to join the European Economic Community, the Meteorological Office first began using Celsius temperature values in its public weather information, following the Fahrenheit values. In October, the Celsius values were listed first, and by the 1st January 1973, when the government entered the EEC and completed its conversion to the metric system, Fahrenheit numbers were only used occasionally.

17th | Ten former game show contestants, all of whom had testified under oath that they had not been given answers in advance of their appearances, pleaded guilty to perjury. The most prominent was former Columbia University instructor Charles Van Doren, who had won $129,000 on the program Twenty One.

th The play Prescription: Murder, by Richard Levinson and William Link, was first presented, with the premiere at the Curran Theatre in San Francisco. Character actor Thomas Mitchell portrayed a dishevelled police detective named Lt. Columbo. When the play was made into a TV movie in 1968, Peter Falk portrayed the detective, and then in the title role of Columbo, one of the recurring segments of the NBC Mystery Movie. Columbo had been seen once before, on the 30th July 1960, in the presentation "Enough Rope", part of The Chevy Mystery Show.

rd Singer Tony Bennett first recorded what would become his signature song, I Left My Heart in San Francisco. Ralph Sharon, who accompanied Bennett's songs on the piano, had been shown the song in 1959 by writers George Cory and Douglass Cross, then put it away in a dresser drawer. Sharon ran across it again when Bennett was invited to perform in San Francisco, and Bennett sang it in December. The song was released as the B-side of Once Upon a Time, and went on to sell two million copies and to win two Grammy Awards.

th The American space probe Ranger 3 was launched from Cape Canaveral at 3:30 pm local time with the objective of duplicating the Soviet feat of landing a satellite on the Moon. Hours later, NASA announced that the Atlas rocket had hurled Ranger 3 into its trajectory too quickly, and that the probe would miss its target by 22,000 miles. Intersecting the Moon's orbit after 50 hours instead of the planned 66 hours, the spacecraft arrived too soon, got no closer than 22,862 miles from the Moon and went into orbit around the sun.

9th The Automobile Manufacturers Association of the U.S. announced that all 1963 model American vehicles would be equipped with amber-coloured turn signals on the front, rather than being the same colour as the headlights, which had been the standard since the signals had first been introduced in 1938. The change was made after the manufacturers had lobbied for the repeal of bans in 25 states against amber-coloured lights.

February

1st   U.S. President Kennedy delivered "the first presidential message entirely devoted to public welfare", proposing that federal aid to the poor be extended to include job training programs and day care for children of working parents.

2nd   The Soviet Union conducted its very first underground nuclear test. Previously, the Soviets had conducted all of its atomic and hydrogen bomb explosions in the atmosphere, including more than fifty since ending moratorium on testing.

4th   The St. Jude Children's Research Hospital opened in Memphis, Tennessee. American comedian Danny Thomas, the hospital's founder, told a crowd of 9,000 that "If I were to die this minute, I would know wh was born... Anyone may dream, but few have realized a dream as gargantuan as this one." Thomas said that he had made a vow in 1937, when he was unemployed and penniless, that he would build a shrine Saint Jude Thaddaeus (patron saint of the lost and helpless) "if I made good". After becoming successful he began raising funds in 1951. Fifty years later, the hospital was treating 7,800 children per year at no cost, and funding cancer research worldwide.

7th   The United States government ban against all U.S.-related Cuban imports (and nearly all exports) went i effect at one minute after midnight. The next day, the Supreme Soviet of the U.S.S.R. approved a $133 million program of military aid to Cuba, after having delayed action on it for four months.

10th   At 8:52 a.m. local time, captured American spy pilot Francis Gary Powers was exchanged for captured Soviet spy Rudolf Abel in Berlin, at the Glienicke Bridge between Wannsee and Potsdam. Powers had be shot down over Russia on the 1st May 1960 while flying a U-2 spy plane. Abel had been arrested in New York on June 21, 1957. Frederic L. Pryor, a 28-year-old American student who had been arrested in East Berlin on the 25th August, was released as part of the deal as well.

11th   Comedian June Carter became a permanent part of the tour of country music singer Johnny Cash, startir with a stop at Des Moines. The two would marry in 1968.

13th   A crowd of between 150,000 and 500,000 people marched in Paris in the first massive protest against th continuing Algerian war, which had gone into its eighth year. The occasion was the funeral ceremony fo five of the nine people who had been killed by police in the Charonne metro station the previous Thursday. With many of the participants walking off of their jobs to protest, business in Paris and much France was brought to a halt.

15th   The Soviet Union restored the death penalty, for rape and for "attacks on police and public order volunteers". Capital punishment had been officially abolished nationwide on May 26, 1947, but graduall reintroduced for various crimes beginning in 1950.

17th   In the North Sea flood of 1962, Hurricane-force winds and heavy rains swept across West Germany's No Sea coast and sent the waters flooding over the seawalls. There were 345 deaths in West Germany, 281 them in Hamburg, when the Elbe River overflowed. An estimated 500,000 people were left homeless.

18th   Two pilots of the French Air Force, described as "renegades", defied orders, broke away from a routine mission over French Algeria, flew their planes across the border into Morocco, and then attacked a rebe camp in the city of Oujda with rockets and machine gun fire. The two, believed to be members of the Organisation armée secrète, then flew their planes to Saïda, Algeria, landed, and deserted.

th Rock musician Chuck Berry reported to the Federal Penitentiary in Terre Haute, Indiana, after his conviction for violating the Mann Act (in 1959) was affirmed. He would, after serving for 20 months of his three-year sentence, be released on the 18th October 1963, and revive his career.

rd Astronaut John Glenn arrived in Cape Canaveral to a hero's welcome and was reunited with his family for the first time since before going into space. U.S. President John F. Kennedy, for whom Cape Canaveral would be renamed during the 1960s, greeted Glenn and personally awarded him the NASA Special Services Medal. Kennedy praised Glenn for "professional skill, unflinching courage and extraordinary ability to perform a most difficult task under physical stress." It was then that Glenn revealed in an interview that the heat shield on his capsule began to break up upon re-entry, the loss of which would have been fatal. Glenn calmly said, "it could have been a bad day for everybody".

th The Judy Garland Show, a one-time special, appeared on CBS and received a 49.5 rating, the highest rating CBS had had for a variety show to that time. The success of the special led to a weekly series in 1963, which was cancelled after a year because of low ratings.

th A group of 15 American Jupiter missiles, with nuclear warheads, became operational at the Izmir U.S. Air Force Base at Çiğli, within range to strike the Soviet Union 1,000 miles away. The presence of American nuclear missiles in a nation bordering the U.S.S.R. would become an issue during the Cuban Missile Crisis, when Soviet nuclear missiles were brought to Cuba, within striking distance of the United States. The missiles were withdrawn from both Turkey and Cuba following the crisis.

rch

st "The Incredible Hulk" was introduced as the first issue of the comic book, by that name, on the shelves of American stores and newsstands. Issue #1 was post-dated to May 1962 in accordance with industry practice.

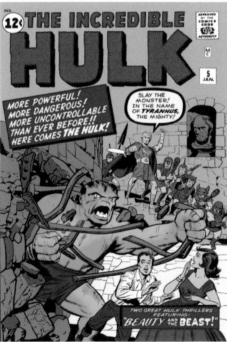

March

5th A B-58 Hustler jet, piloted by U.S. Air Force Captain Robert Sowers, and a crew of two, set three new records by flying from Los Angeles to New York in 2 hours, 01:15, and then back again in 2 hours, 15:02. The sonic boom, from the jet's speed of more than 1,000 mph, broke windows in Riverside, California and Chillicothe, Missouri when it accelerated at 30,000 feet and during a refuelling, and emergency calls were made in cities beneath the flight path. The USAF received more than 10,000 complaints as a result of the flight.

6th U.S. Patent #3,023,527 was granted to Wayne Leek and Charles Morse for the Remington Nylon 66, a rifle which required no added lubricants because the stock was made of the nylon variant Zytel.

9th Three babies at the Binghamton General Hospital in Binghamton, New York died suddenly of heart failure. Three more were dead the next day, with four others in critical condition, and all had abnormally high sodium levels. The deaths of the six infants, three boys and three girls, who ranged in age from 3 days to months old, were traced to a nurse's mistaken placement of salt, three days earlier, into a sugar container used for the making of baby formula. Ironically, the discovery was made by another nurse who broke hospital rules when she made herself a cup of coffee in the formula room. The deaths were subsequently ruled as accidental.

11th Jackie Kennedy, the First Lady of the United States, had a 33 minute long audience with Pope John XXIII Rome, one of the longest private audiences ever granted by the Pope. She left that evening for a visit to India.

13th Operation Northwood's, a top secret proposal to use American funding for terror attacks within the United States, was presented to U.S. Secretary of Defence Robert McNamara by Army General L. L. Lemnitzer, Chairman of the Joint Chiefs of Staff. With the goal of carrying out violent acts that could be blamed on the Communist government in Cuba in order to get support for an invasion, the proposals included exploding an empty U.S. Navy ship in Guantanamo Bay and creating a false list of casualties; and faking an attack, to be blamed on Cuba, on a chartered airliner flying from the United States. The most incredible proposal was to simulate a "Communist Cuban terror campaign in the Miami area, other Florida cities, and even in Washington", including "exploding a few plastic bombs in carefully chosen spots", and directed against Cuban refugees "even to the point of wounding." The plan, which would be declassified in 2001, was vetoed by McNamara before it reached President Kennedy.

16th Flying Tiger Line Flight 739, a Lockheed Constellation airliner carrying 96 Army personnel and a crew of 11 to the Philippines, disappeared at 1:30 am local time (1530 GMT on the 15th March) after taking off from Guam. Despite a massive search of the Pacific Ocean, no trace of the airliner, nor the 107 persons on board, was ever found.

17th The annual Gaelic Games competition was televised for the first time, as RTÉ broadcast the finals of the Railway Cup, hurling championship of the Gaelic Athletic Association. Leinster beat defending champion Munster by a score of 1 goal, 11 points to 1 goal, nine points, equivalent to 14–12.

19th Bob Dylan, the debut album of singer-songwriter Bob Dylan, was released by Columbia Records. The record sold only a few hundred copies in its first six months. The next year, Dylan would become famous with the best-selling "Blowin' in the Wind".

21st The first Taco Bell restaurant was opened, as entrepreneur Glen Bell began the restaurant chain in Downey, California.

nd FBI Director J. Edgar Hoover met at the White House with John F. Kennedy, to advise him about what findings from a wiretap revealed. Not only was Hoover aware that President Kennedy was conducting an extramarital affair with Judith Exner, Hoover advised that Ms. Exner was also romantically involved with organized crime figures Sam Giancana and Johnny Roselli, and Frank Sinatra. After the meeting, Kennedy called Exner to terminate the relationship. The affair would not become public knowledge until Congressional hearings were held in 1975.

rd The first noble gas compound was created by British chemist Neil Bartlett in Vancouver, when he created xenon hexafluoroplatinate ("XePtF6) from a reaction of xenon and platinum hexafluoride.

th World welterweight boxing champion Benny Paret lost his title, and his life, to former champ Emile Griffith in a bout at Madison Square Garden in New York City. In the 12th round, Griffith unleashed a torrent of punches as Paret was on the ropes, and referee Ruby Goldstein stopped the fight. Peret sagged, and then collapsed. Paret, who had knocked down Griffith at the end of the sixth round, was taken to Roosevelt Hospital, where he underwent emergency brain surgery. He never regained consciousness and died on the 2nd April.

7th New York State Governor Nelson Rockefeller signed legislation to allow the Port of New York Authority to begin construction of the World Trade Centre in Manhattan.

9th Comedian Jack Paar concluded his last appearance as host of "The Jack Paar Show" then known informally as "The Tonight Show" on NBC, after five years. The guests on the last show were Jack E. Leonard, Alexander King, Robert Merrill and Buddy Hackett. Among those appearing in taped farewell messages were Richard Nixon, Robert Kennedy, Billy Graham, Bob Hope and Jack Benny. Hugh Downs was the announcer, and Jose Melis led the band. The show would continue as "The Tonight Show" the following week, with guest hosts, until Johnny Carson took over on the 1st October 1962. Paar's last regular appearance was on a Thursday. The final show, on Friday 30th March 1962 was a "Best Of Paar" rerun. Jack Paar returned to television later that year, in November, as host of the Friday night "The Jack Paar Program"

1st A tornado killed 15 people in the city of Milton, Florida and injured more than 75.

April

3rd As the Algerian War for Independence came to an end, European OAS gunmen near Algiers carried out a terrorist attack against a Muslims hospital in the suburb of Beau-Fraisier, killing nine. The 15 former Fre Army soldiers, armed with sub-machine guns, rushed past hospital employees and targeted bedridden patients, then exited. Most of the victims had been hospitalized for months, due to ailments unrelated t the war.

6th The United Steel Workers of America and steel manufacturers agreed to a new contract, brokered by th U.S. Department of Labour, in which the union reduced its demands for a wage increase from 17 cents t 10 cents an hour, based upon the White House's determination to hold down prices. Four days later, the steel makers raised their prices anyway. A furious President Kennedy forced U.S. Steel and other companies to rescind the increase on the 13th April.

9th The United States Marine Corps' involvement in the Vietnam War began when HMM-362 arrived at Soc Trang south of Saigon (South Vietnam).

10th U.S. Steel Chairman Roger Blough informed President Kennedy, at a 5:45 pm meeting at the White Hous that the largest steel manufacturer in the world was planning to raise its prices by six dollars per ton at 12:01 a.m. Kennedy reportedly told Blough, "You've made a terrible mistake." As Blough's press release reached American newspapers, the President announced that he would have a special press conference on Thursday.

11th As three other American steelmakers announced a price hike, President Kennedy denounced "Big Steel" a press conference "with the strongest language he has levelled at anyone or anything since becoming President". In March, the U.S. Department of Labour had helped mediate a contract between the Unitec Steelworkers of America and the companies, with the union agreeing to a smaller wage increase in orde to prevent a price rise.

13th U.S. Secretary of Labour Arthur J. Goldberg met privately in New York City with U.S. Steel Chairman Rog M. Blough, and outlined the steps that the Kennedy administration would take if the steel price increase continued. At 3:05 pm, Kaiser Steel rescinded its price increase, followed by Bethlehem Steel at 3:21 pm The largest of the companies, U.S. Steel, capitulated at 5:25 pm, followed by Republic Steel (5:57), Pittsburgh Steel (6:26), Jones & Laughlin (6:37), National Steel (7:33) and Youngstown Sheet & Tube (9:0

14th Cuba's new revolutionary socialist prime minister Fidel Castro, "in an unexpected burst of generosity", allowed 60 of the 1,179 Bay of Pigs invaders to be released from Principe Prison for reasons of health, ar to be flown from Havana to Miami on a Pan American World Airways jet, without conditions.

16th Folk singer Bob Dylan, who had recently released his debut album, made the first public performance of what would become his signature song, "Blowin' in the Wind". The setting was Gerde's Folk City, a "jazz club" located at 11 West 4th Street in New York City's Greenwich Village.

18th The first underground ballistic missile base in the U.S. became operational, with the delivery of the first nine Titan I missiles, to silos at Lowry Air Force Base, in, Colorado. By the 28th September all 54 Titans would be activated at bases in five western U.S. states. However, all of the Titan I group would be removed by the 1st April 1965 when they were made obsolete by the more efficient Atlas ICBM rockets, which did not have to be raised from the silo in order to be fuelled and armed.

st | A flight formation of 24 U.S. Air Force and U.S. Navy jets, part of the opening ceremonies of the Seattle World's Fair, ended in tragedy. One of the F-102 Dagger jet fighters experienced flight trouble. The pilot ejected safely, but the jet crashed into a residential neighbourhood at the suburb of Mountlake Terrace, Washington, destroying two homes and killing an elderly couple. A five-member family that normally resided in the other home had gone on Easter vacation to avoid the traffic associated with the fair opening.

rd | The American Ranger 4 satellite was launched at 2:50 pm local time from Cape Canaveral, with the objective of gathering data from the Moon. A few hours later, ground control found that the satellite would be unable to keep still enough to provide useful information. One NASA official commented, "All we've got is an idiot with a radio signal."

th | "We have created the first synthetic thunderstorm in space", NASA scientist Dr. Wernher Von Braun announced, after an American Saturn rocket released 95 tons of water into the ionosphere. At an altitude of 65 miles, explosives on the rocket were detonated by ground control, creating a 25 mile wide cloud of ice that was visible from Florida. Von Braun announced that electrical charges were detected in the ice mass.

th | The A-12 Blackbird, prototype for the Lockheed SR-71 Blackbird jet airplane, made its first flight, piloted by Lou Schalk, who took off and landed at the Groom Lake base in Nevada.

| A-12 Blackbird | Groom Lake | Lockheed SR-71 Blackbird |

th | Norway's Parliament, the Storting, voted 113–37 in favour of Norway applying to join the European Economic Community. France would veto the application later in the year, but Norway would join the Common Market in 1972.

th | In one of the largest White House state dinners in modern times, the President and Mrs. Kennedy hosted 173 scientists, educators and writers, including 49 Nobel Prize laureates from the Western Hemisphere. President Kennedy made the famous remark, "I think this is the most extraordinary collection of talent, of human knowledge ever gathered at the White House, with the possible exception of when Thomas Jefferson dined alone." Dr. Linus Pauling, winner of the 1954 prize in chemistry, picketed outside of the White House in an anti-nuclear demonstration earlier in the day, then went inside to join the President for dinner. On greeting Dr. Pauling, Kennedy said, "I'm glad you decided to come inside."

th | NASA test pilot Joe Walker set a new altitude record for a fixed wing aircraft, flying an X-15 jet up to 246,700 feet (75,190 meters).

May

1st The Dayton Hudson Corporation opened the first of its Target discount stores. The store (now a "Super Target") is located at 1515 West County Road B, in the St. Paul suburb of Roseville, Minnesota.

2nd An OAS car bomb exploded at the docks of Algiers, killing 96 people. The deaths of 14 other people and the injury of 147 overall made the occasion "the bloodiest single day in the modern history of Algeria's capital".

3rd The Mikawashima train crash killed 160 people in Japan in the collision involving three separate trains near Tokyo. Engineer Norifumi Minakami drove a freight train through a red signal and sideswiped a commuter train. As surviving passengers climbed out of that train, a third train ran through them, and then plunged over an embankment.

5th Seattle businessman Stanley McDonald inaugurated a cruise ship service that would eventually become Princess Cruises, starting with the departure of the Canadian steamer SS Yarmouth from San Francisco for the first of 17 ten-day cruises to the 1962 Seattle World's Fair and back. After a successful six-month lease of the Yarmouth, McDonald would spend more than three years in making plans for the Princess Cruise line (which would be made famous by The Love Boat television series) on a regular series of winter tours from Los Angeles to Acapulco, starting at the end of 1965. "Yarmouth Cruises, Inc."

6th The first nuclear explosion to be caused by an American ballistic missile, rather than by a bomb dropped from an aircraft or at a fixed site, was accomplished at Christmas Island, 1,200 miles from its launch site. Previous ICBM tests had been done without a nuclear warhead. The USS Ethan Allen fired the armed Polaris A-2 missile, from underwater, to its target.

7th Detroit became the first city in the United States to use traffic cameras and electronic signs to regulate the flow of traffic. The pilot program began with 14 television cameras along a 3.2-mile stretch of the John C. Lodge Freeway, between the Davison Expressway and Interstate 94.

9th The Sikorsky S-64 Skycrane helicopter, capable of lifting 20,000 pounds (over 9,000 kg), made its first flight.

In accepting the Sylvanus Thayer Award, retired General Douglas MacArthur delivered his memorable "Duty, Honour, Country" speech to West Point cadets. The 82-year-old MacArthur delivered the 30-minute address from memory and without notes, and a recording of the remarks would be released as a record album later.

Nine men, on a fishing trip, died in shark-infested waters after their boat sank off the coast of Newport Beach, California. Chester McMain of Norwalk was taking the Happy Jack on its first voyage when it ran into rough weather. Though they were wearing life jackets, the sharks apparently pulled them underwater. Searchers on the fishing boat Mardic located six bodies the next day, with sharks swimming around the group.

The last execution of an American for armed robbery, without homicide, took place in Texas as an African-American man was given the electric chair.

The first 1,800 United States Marines dispatched to Southeast Asia, troops of the 3rd Marine Expeditionary Brigade, arrived at Bangkok to guard Thailand's border with Laos. The Thai government had given permission for 5,000 American troops to stay.

Marilyn Monroe made her last significant public appearance, singing "Happy Birthday, Mr. President" at a birthday party for President John F. Kennedy at Madison Square Garden. The event was part of a fundraiser to pay off the Democratic Party's four million-dollar debt remaining from Kennedy's 1960 presidential campaign. Monroe was stitched into a $12,000 dress "made of nothing but beads" and wore nothing underneath as she appeared at the request of Peter Lawford; President Kennedy thanked her afterward, joking, "I can now retire from politics after having had 'Happy Birthday' sung to me in such a sweet, wholesome way."

May

20th | The first specifically built coronary care unit in the world opened at the Bethany Hospital in Kansas City, Missouri, under the planning of cardiologist Dr. Hughes Day. Other CCUs followed in Toronto, Sydney, N York and Philadelphia, and by 1970, most major hospitals had units designed to treat heart attacks.

23rd | The first successful reattachment (replantation) of a severed limb was accomplished by Dr. Ronald A. M at Massachusetts General Hospital in Boston. Everett Knowles, a 12-year-old boy, had had his right arm severed at the shoulder by a freight train. A year after the limb was saved, Everett could move all five fingers and bend his wrist, and by 1965, he was again playing baseball and tennis.

26th | Acker Bilk's "Stranger On The Shore" became the first British recording to reach number one in the US Billboard Hot 100.

30th | The 1962 FIFA World Cup began in Chile.

June

3rd | Air France Flight 007, chartered as the Chateau de Sully, overran the runway on take-off from Orly Airpc in Paris, at 12:29 pm local time, killing all 122 passengers and 8 of the 10 crew members. Two flight attendants survived. Most (106 of the 122) of the victims were cultural and civic leaders of the Atlanta A Association, returning home from a tour of Europe. The Boeing 707 crashed through an airport fence an into the woods near the village of Villeneuve-le-Roi.

4th | The 1962 Isle of Man TT races were held at the Snaefell Mountain Course. Winners included Luigi Taveri Derek Minter and Ernst Degner.

5th | The Amazing Spider-Man, created by Stan Lee and Steve Ditko, was introduced by Marvel Comics with t publication of Amazing Fantasy#15. With a cover date of August 1962, the issue was placed on newsstar on the 5th June 1962, according to the copyright renewal filed in 1990.

8th | Marilyn Monroe was fired by 20th Century Fox because of her frequent absences from the filming of the movie Something's Got to Give. Over a course of seven weeks of shooting, she had only appeared on fiv days.

11th | Frank Morris, John Anglin and Clarence Anglin became the last prisoners to escape from the Alcatraz Isla federal penitentiary. They were not recaptured, nor were their bodies ever located by searchers, and we presumed to have drowned. The Alcatraz prison Clint Eastwood would later portray Morris in the 1979 f Escape from Alcatraz.

12th | Three days before his high school graduation, 18-year-old George Lucas survived a near-fatal car crash caused by a fellow student. Lucas would abandon a dream to become a race car driver, and went on to become a successful filmmaker.

13th | Lee Harvey Oswald arrived back in the United States on the Dutch cruise ship S.S. Maasdam, after more than two years away in Russia. Oswald, who would be accused of killing U.S. President Kennedy less than 18 months later.

Brazil beat Czechoslovakia 3–1 to win the 1962 FIFA World Cup Final, played in Santiago, Chile. Czechoslovakia was ahead 1-0 on a goal by Josef Masopust, eleven minutes into the game and the teams were tied 1-1 at halftime. Zito hit a goal from Brazil at the 69th minute for a 2-1 edge. At 78 minutes, In the second half, Czechoslovakian goalie Viliam Schrojf was blinded by the sun, allowing Brazil's Vavá to score the final goal for the 3-1 win.

The second phase of building the Berlin Wall was commenced. Not only was the outer wall along the border with West Berlin increased, but buildings along the border were torn down in order to clear an area at that extended at least 30 meters further from the border. The in-between area was then filled with land mines and other deterrents to escape.

Actress Sophia Loren and her husband, producer Carlo Ponti, were ordered to stand trial on bigamy charges.

After IBM rejected the idea of 32-year-old employee H. Ross Perot, to sell computer programs along with its equipment, Perot quit and invested $1,000 of his savings to create Electronic Data Systems (EDS). When Medicare was created in 1965, EDS contracted with two states to process the claims, turning the company into a multibillion-dollar corporation and making a billionaire of Perot.

John Henry Faulk, an American disc jockey whose career had been ruined by false charges that he was a Communist, was awarded $3.5 million by a New York jury.

RKO Phonevision, a pay TV service operated by Zenith Radio Company, began a pay-per-view service in Hartford, Connecticut, sending scrambled signals in addition to the regular programming on WHCT Channel 18. On the first night, subscribers with Phonevision decoders (and one dollar) were able to watch the recent (1960) film Sunrise at Campobello with no commercial interruptions. The service never attracted enough subscribers to break even, and ended on the 31st January 1969.

Unrestricted immigration, of British Empire subjects, to the United Kingdom was curtailed as the Commonwealth Immigrants Act 1962 took effect, putting a quota on how many government vouchers would be issued for each nation. Restrictions would become stricter in 1971.

The last soldiers of the French Foreign Legion left Algeria.

1st | Bruce McLaren won the 1962 Reims Grand Prix. McClaren of New Zealand, a former rugby player turned race car driver, finished the 250-mile course in 2 hours, 2 seconds.

2nd | The first Walmart store was opened as Wal-Mart Discount City in Rogers, Arkansas, by Sam Walton. By 1970, there would be 38 Wal-Mart stores. After 50 years, there were more than 9,766 stores in 27 countries, and 11,766 by mid-2019.

6th | The 320 feet (98 m) deep Sedan Crater, measuring 1,280 feet (390 m) in diameter, was created in less th a split-second in Nye County, Nevada with an underground nuclear test. The fallout exposed 13 million Americans to radiation; regular monthly tours are now given of the crater, which ceased being radioacti after less than a year.

9th | In the Starfish Prime test, the United States exploded a 1.4 megaton hydrogen bomb in outer space, sending the warhead on a Titan missile to an altitude of 248 miles over Johnston Island. The first two attempts at exploding a nuclear missile above the Earth had failed. The flash was visible in Hawaii, 750 miles away, and scientists discovered the destructive effects of the first major manmade electromagneti pulse (EMP), as a surge of electrons burned out streetlights, blew fuses, and disrupted communications. Increasing radiation in some places one hundredfold, the EMP damaged at least ten orbiting satellites beyond repair.

12th | The first telephone signals carried by satellite were made from by engineers between Goonhilly in the U and Andover, Maine in the U.S.

14th | In the third match of the rugby league Test series between Australia and Great Britain, held at Sydney Cricket Ground, a controversial last-minute Australian try and the subsequent conversion resulted in an 18–17 win for Australia.

15th | Radiation killed all six animals, sent up 24 hours earlier by NASA, in the first test of whether astronauts could safely endure prolonged exposure to cosmic rays. The two monkeys and four hamsters had been inside a space capsule that had been kept at an altitude of 131,000 feet by a balloon.

18th | The largest space vehicle, up to that time, began orbiting the Earth, after the communications satellite " Shot" was launched by the United States. After going aloft, the silvery balloon was inflated to its full size a sphere with a diameter of 135 feet.

20th | The world's first regular passenger hovercraft service was introduced, as the VA-3 began the 20-mile run between Rhyl (in Wales) and Wallasey (in England).

24th | The first successful use of a biological valve in human heart surgery was performed by Dr. Donald Nixon Ross in London, with a sub coronary implantation of an aortic allograft.

25th | "Skyphone" service, permitting airline passengers to make telephone calls while in flight, was inaugurate The first call was made from American Airlines Flight 941 en route from New York to Cincinnati, from stewardess Hope Patterson to the Associated Press.

26th | The first Soviet nuclear missiles were unloaded in Cuba at the port of Mariel; their discovery would precipitate the Cuban Missile Crisis.

7th Jess Oliver (Oliver Jsesperson) applied for the patent for the Ampeg B-15 Portaflex portable bass amplifier, which would become the most popular bass amplifier in the world for bands; the patent would be granted on the 11th May 1965.

8th The Bundesliga, the national league of West Germany's top professional soccer football teams, was created by a 103–26 vote of delegates to the German Football Association (DFB) convention at Dortmund. The Bundesliga would begin its first season on August 24, 1963 with 16 teams out of 46 applicants.

0th Marilyn Monroe made a final telephone call to the U.S. Justice Department, six days before her death. Monroe had been a regular caller to U.S. Attorney General Robert F. Kennedy, and historians speculate that he told her during the eight-minute phone call that they could no longer see each other. Monroe's phone records would be confiscated by the FBI, but Kennedy's phone logs would be donated to the National Archives after his death.

ugust

3rd President John F. Kennedy made the decision to break ties with singer Frank Sinatra after his brother, U.S. Attorney General Robert F. Kennedy, delivered him a report detailing Sinatra's connections with organized crime. Sinatra, reportedly, was so enraged by the President's decision to no longer visit the singer's home in Palm Springs, California, that he took a sledgehammer and personally destroyed a landing pad built to accommodate visits by the presidential helicopter, Marine One.

4th Marilyn Monroe took the fatal overdose of Nembutal pills at her home at 12305 5th Helena Drive in Brentwood in Los Angeles, apparently at some point between a 7:15 phone call from her former stepson, Joe DiMaggio, Jr., and a 7:30 pm call from actor Peter Lawford. The pills interacted with a dosage of chloral hydrate already in her body, and she was in a coma by 10:00 pm.

7th Patsy Cline released her final studio album, Sentimentally Yours, seven months before her death in a plane crash.

3th On the first anniversary of the creation of the Berlin Wall, three minutes of silence were supposed to be observed at noon in West Berlin. Instead, angry crowds began hurling stones across the border at police in East Berlin, who responded by firing a water cannon across the Wall and into the crowd. After more stones were thrown by the Western protesters, tear gas grenades were fired from East Berlin, after which West Berlin riot police sent their own tear gas across the border. The clash ended after an hour, and there were no serious injuries.

4th In the Plymouth Mail Robbery, robbers armed with submachineguns held up a U.S. Mail truck near Plymouth, Massachusetts, and heisted its $1,500,000 cargo that had been en route to the Federal Reserve Bank in Boston. The truck was flagged down by a man dressed as a police officer, and two cars pulled out from side roads. The caper was financed by mobster Gennaro "Jerry" Angiulo and carried out under the direction of John "Red" Kelley. Kelley would later arrange for the murder of six of the participants in the plot, would later avoid prison by becoming a witness against his fellow criminals, and, after being relocated by the federal witness protection program, would eventually die of natural causes.

5th South Africa legalized the sale of beer, wine and liquor to Africans and Asians for the first time. Previously, the privilege had been limited to White people only.

August

17th Peter Fechter, 18, was killed by East German border guards as he attempted to cross the Berlin Wall int West Berlin. Fechter's death has been described as "the most notorious incident of all" in the 27-year history of the Wall, because Fechter slowly bled to death from his bullet wounds, in front of newspaper photographers and hundreds of spectators who were unable to assist him, and East German guards wh refused to approach him until he died an hour later. In 1996, indictments would be returned against the two former guards, Rolf Friedrich and Erich Schreiber, who had shot Fechter. They would be convicted c manslaughter on the 5th March 1997, and placed on probation.

21st The source of the anti-cancer drug taxol (paclitaxel) was discovered by a team of botanists, led by Dr. Arthur Barclay, who collected bark from a specific type of Pacific yew tree, Taxus brevifolia Nutt, in the Gifford Pinchot National Forest. Taxol, developed from the extract of the bark, is now used in treatmen ovarian and breast cancer.

24th In the most dramatic attack on Cuba since the Bay of Pigs Invasion the year before, a suburb of Havana was shelled from speedboats operated by the Cuban exile terrorist group Directorio Estudiantile. Operating from a 31-foot boat, the attackers, led by Manuel Salvat fired 60 artillery shells at buildings ir Miramar, an upscale section of the Havana suburb of Playa. Nine rooms of the Icar Hostel, formerly the Hotel Rosita de Hornedo, were damaged, and 20 people were injured. The boat departed after seven minutes.

27th NASA launched the Mariner 2 space probe toward Venus, with lift-off from Florida at 1:58 am local time As the first successful mission to another planet, Mariner 2 would reach the second planet on Decembe 14, 1962, gathering data for 42 minutes and approaching within 21,600 miles (34,752 km). The launch came a month after the failed American launch of Mariner 1 to Venus, and three days after the Soviet launch of Sputnik 19 to Venus.

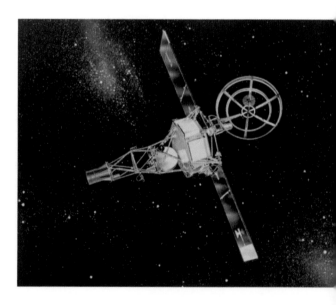

29th Photographs by an American U-2 spyplane over Cuba first revealed the presence there of Soviet SA-2 missiles, for anti-aircraft defence. Offensive, nuclear-armed missiles would not be discovered in Cuba ur later flights, precipitating the Cuban Missile Crisis.

30th The Supremes recorded their fourth single, "Let Me Go the Right Way", at Studio A of "Hitsville U.S.A.", Motown Records recording studios at 2648 West Grand Boulevard in Detroit.

st | A 7.1 magnitude earthquake in northwest Iran destroyed 91 villages and killed 12,225 people. The epicentre was near Buin Zahra in the Qazvin Province.

th | The closing ceremony of the 1962 Asian Games was held in Jakarta, Indonesia, following an attack on India's embassy by 1,000 rioters. Earlier, Asian Games Federation Vice-President G. D. Sondhi had announced that he was seeking to have the executive council declare that the competition was not part of the name "Asian Games", because AGF members Israel and Nationalist China (Taiwan) had had their teams excluded.

th | The Cuban Missile Crisis began as the first consignment of Soviet R-12 (called SS-4 by NATO) offensive missiles arrived in Cuba, on board the freighter Omsk. The medium range ballistic missiles, which could be fitted with nuclear warheads and could strike targets in the U.S. within 2,000 km or 1,300 miles of Cuba.

th | Jack Nicklaus won the first "World Series of Golf", a made-for-television exhibition organized by the NBC television network as a competition between the champions of the four major professional golf tournaments. With a 138 on 36 holes, Nicklaus (winner of the U.S. Open) won the $50,000 first prize by finishing four strokes ahead of ahead of Masters and British Open champion Arnold Palmer and PGA Championship winner Gary Player, who tied at 139.

th | President John F. Kennedy, in a speech at the football stadium of Rice University in Houston, reaffirmed that the U.S. would put a man on the Moon by the end of the decade. On hand were 40,000 people, mostly students. Kennedy had declared, on the 25th May 1961, his belief that the nation should commit to a manned moon landing, which would be achieved on the 10th July 1969.

th | The first Soviet medium-range missiles were deployed in Cuba, a week after their arrival. On the same day, American electronic intelligence detected that Soviet high-altitude surface-to-air missiles had become operational. An SA-2 (or S-75) Dvina missile had downed the U-2 spy plane flown by Francis Gary Powers in 1960, and the weapons, located near the port of Mariel, were capable of stopping further American attempts to verify a missile build-up.

th | A full-scale mock-up of the Boeing X-20 Dyna-Soar spaceplane was unveiled for reporters in Las Vegas, where the Air Force Association was holding its annual convention, and the six pilots who would be the first to fly the X-20 were introduced. "Technical men familiar with sketches and photographs of the X-20 were startled by the vicious ugliness" of the plane, the Associated Press reported, noting that "With its upturned wingtips and long snout, the X-20 looks like its designer had somehow managed to cross a manta ray with a shark." "Our Black Dyna-Soar Shows Its Ugly Snout" The Dyna-Soar project, scheduled for a 1965 launch, would be cancelled after cost overruns, and none were ever built.

nd | Autostrada 1, a 125-mile long superhighway between Rome and Naples, was opened to traffic. Travel time between the two Italian cities was cut almost in half, from 3 1/2 hours to two hours.

rd | The Jetsons - George, Jane, Judy and Elroy - were introduced in a primetime cartoon of the same name at 7:30 pm Eastern time on the ABC television network. Despite having only 24 episodes, the science fiction show, about a family living about 100 years in the future, would be rerun for 23 years until new episodes were commissioned for a syndicated revival in 1985.

September

25th | Sonny Liston and Floyd Patterson fought for the world heavyweight boxing title in Chicago. Liston made history by being the first man ever to knock out a reigning heavyweight champion in the first round, downing the titleholder in 2 minutes and 6 seconds.

26th | The Beverly Hillbillies, a television situation comedy about a poor Ozark Mountains family who became multi-millionaires after oil was found on their land, began a nine-year run on the CBS network, with the first episode premiering at 9:00 pm Eastern time. UPI television critic Rick Du Brow wrote the next day that the series "is going to be a smash hit" in that it was similar in premise to TV program The Real McCoy's, added that "The nicest thing I can say... is that it is really not like 'The Real McCoy's'... The McCoy's are a civilized rural clan; these new hillbillies make L'il Abner and his mob look like a bunch of sophisticates. Within three weeks, it was the most-watched series on American television, and stayed at #1 in its first two seasons. The show had 274 episodes, with the final one broadcast on the 23rd March 1971.

29th | My Fair Lady ended its Broadway run after more than six years and 2,717 performances, a Broadway record that would stand until surpassed later by Hello, Dolly!

October

1st | Four Soviet Foxtrot submarines, armed with nuclear torpedoes, departed bases on the Kola Peninsula in anticipation of a confrontation with the United States over Cuba.

3rd | A steam boiler explosion, at a New York Telephone Company building in Manhattan, killed twenty-one people and injured 70. The blast happened at 12:07 pm while employees were dining in the building's cafeteria, sending the boiler from the basement into the cafeteria, then out through a wall.

4th | The first nuclear missile in Cuba was installed by the Soviet Union, as a warhead was attached to an R-1 rocket.

6th | The U.S. Marine Corps and U.S. Navy suffered their first helicopter fatalities in Vietnam when a Marine Corps UH-34 Seahorse crashed 15 miles (24 km) from Tam Ky, South Vietnam, killing five Marines and two Navy personnel.

9ᵗʰ The MCC cricket team arrived in Fremantle, Western Australia, to begin its 1962–63 tour.

12ᵗʰ The Bridge of the Americas was opened in Panama exactly three years after construction began. With clearance of over 200 feet, it was the first to allow traffic to cross uninterrupted between Central America and South America because the bridge did not need to be moved. 12ᵗʰ October was chosen for the start and finish of construction in honour of the 12ᵗʰ October 1492 landfall of Christopher Columbus.

13ᵗʰ A treaty between France and the tiny principality of Monaco took effect, with the objective of stopping the practice by wealthy French citizens of moving their residence to Monaco to avoid high taxes. Under Article 7, any French person who had not been "habitually resident in Monaco for five years" would be required to pay French taxes.

17ᵗʰ Nick Holonyak, Jr., and S. F. Bevacqua, both engineers with the General Electric Company, announced their discovery of the physical process that would make the light emitting diode — the LED — practical, by submitting their paper "Coherent (Visible) Light Emission from Ga(As1–xPx) Junctions" to the weekly journal Applied Physics Letters, which would publish the work in its December 1 issue. Although silicon diodes had been able to generate light on the infrared spectrum, it took a specific alloy of gallium (Ga), arsenic (As) and phosphorus (P) to generate visible light; initially, LEDs were limited to red light, but the GaAsP system would later be perfected with nitrates to produce other primary colours, making it possible to generate the full spectrum.

19ᵗʰ President Kennedy met with the Joint Chiefs of Staff to discuss the military options for responding to the missiles in Cuba. USAF Chief of Staff General Curtis LeMay advocated bombing of the missile sites in Cuba, while Defence Secretary Robert McNamara recommended a blockade of ships approaching the island. Ultimately, Kennedy, who would spend the day at scheduled speeches in Ohio and Illinois, would opt to blockade Cuba rather than to start a war.

23ʳᵈ As the American blockade of Cuba from Soviet ships was set, the 450 ships of the U.S. Atlantic Fleet and 200,000 personnel prepared for a confrontation, including defence if the Soviets tried an airlift over the blockade. The Soviet freighter Polotavia was identified as the first ship that would reach the quarantine line.

25ᵗʰ At 6:50 a.m., the American destroyers USS Joseph P. Kennedy, Jr. and the USS John R. Pierce made the first enforcement of the blockade, stopping and boarding the Soviet-chartered ship Marcula, 400 miles from Cuba. After spending two hours searching the Marcula and determining that its cargo of trucks, paper, sulphur and auto parts provided no threat, the Navy allowed the ship to proceed with its cargo.

27ᵗʰ Hours later, the Soviet submarine B-59 was detected by U.S. Navy destroyers in the Atlantic Ocean, and one of the ships began dropping explosive depth charges to force the sub to surface. Thirty years later, a communications intelligence officer on the B-59, would report that the Captain Valentin Savitsky ordered a nuclear-armed torpedo to be armed for firing at the U.S. ships, and that the second-in-command, Vasily Arkhipov, persuaded Savitsky to surface instead.

29ᵗʰ The bodies of Lt. Günther Mollenhauer, and several other Germans shot down over the UK during the Second World War, were disinterred from a local cemetery for re-burial at Cannock Chase German war cemetery.

November

1st | The United States resumed its arms blockade of ships bound for Cuba, after a two-day suspension during which negotiations had taken place. Meanwhile, the Soviet Union began dismantling its missiles there.

2nd | A final agreement was reached between the Soviet Union and the United States reached on the terms for Soviet removal of nuclear missiles from Cuba and American verification. U.S. President John F. Kennedy announced the plan, resolving the Cuban Missile Crisis on television that evening.

4th | The United States conducted an atmospheric nuclear test for the last time, and all of its tests since then have been made underground. The Soviet Union would halt atmospheric testing less than two months later, the last explosion being on Christmas Day. The last atmospheric test ever would be by China on the 16th October 1980.

7th | Soviet Premier Khrushchev announced that the withdrawal of Soviet missiles from Cuba was complete. By agreement of the two superpowers, the United States Navy searched all Soviet vessels leaving Cuba to ensure that the missiles were being transported back to the U.S.S.R., and over the next three days, all 42 ballistic missiles had passed through the inspection bringing an end to the Cuban Missile Crisis.

12th | Two hand surgeons, Dr. Harold E. Kleinert and Dr. Mort Kasdan, performed the first successful revascularization of a severed digit (in this case, a partially amputated thumb) on a human patient, reconnecting the dorsal veins in order to restore function to the hand. The procedure took place at the University of Louisville hospital.

15th | Archie Moore, who had reigned as boxing's world light heavyweight champion between 1952 and 1962, fought unbeaten challenger Cassius Clay (later Muhammad Ali) in Los Angeles. Clay, who had gained a reputation as "the Louisville Lip who calls the round for a knockout and makes it come true", predicted that he would win in four rounds and knocked Moore out in the fourth.

Archie Moore

Cassius Clay

th | At Chantilly, Virginia, 26 miles from Washington, D.C., U.S. President Kennedy dedicated Dulles International Airport, named after the late U.S. Secretary of State John Foster Dulles.

rd | United Airlines Flight 297, a Vickers Viscount 754D, struck a flock of whistling swans while making an approach to Washington, D.C., and crashed north of Ellicott City, Maryland, killing all 17 people on board. One of the swans collided with the left horizontal stabilizer on the tail section, causing the plane to go out of control and into the ground.

th | The first Boeing 727 was rolled out from its hangar in Seattle, and would be flown for the first time on the 9th February 1963, with Eastern Airlines putting it into commercial service a year later.

th | An agreement was signed between Britain and France to develop the Concorde supersonic airliner. Only 14 would ever enter service.

cember

st | The 1962 British Empire and Commonwealth Games came to an end, in Perth, Western Australia.

th | The first Test match of the 1962–63 Ashes series ended in a draw at Brisbane Cricket Ground.

th | The space program of the People's Republic of China suffered a setback when 200 kilograms of a solid rocket fuel mixture exploded during preparation, killing four technicians.

th | The Atlas supercomputer, the most powerful in the world up to that time (with 576 KB storage), was dedicated at the University of Manchester. It was the first system ever designed for multiprogramming, and would be used for the next decade.

th | David Lean's epic film Lawrence of Arabia, featuring Peter O' Toole, Omar Sharif, Alec Guinness, Jack Hawkins, and Anthony Quinn had its worldwide première as a special showing for Queen Elizabeth II and invited guests in London.

th | The last execution in Canada took place at Don Jail, Toronto, when Ronald Turpin, 29, and Arthur Lucas, 54, convicted for separate murders, were hanged at the same time. Turpin had shot a constable in Toronto in February, while Lucas, an African-American from Detroit, had murdered two people in 1961. Years later, Chaplain Cyril Everitt would reveal in an interview that "The hanging was bungled. Turpin died clean, but Lucas' head was torn right off. It was hanging just by the sinews of the neck."; on the 14th July 1976, Canada would abolish the death penalty by a vote of 131–124 in the House of Commons.

th | The Osmond's made their national television debut, singing on The Andy Williams Show, and would appear the following week on Williams's Christmas special. The brothers from Provo, Utah, ranging in age from 7 to 13, were Alan, Wayne, Merrill and Jay Osmond singing two songs. Their younger brother, Donny Osmond, would debut the following Christmas.

th | The Mona Lisa, by Leonardo da Vinci, was assessed for insurance purposes at USD$100 million, before the painting was scheduled to begin its tour the United States for several months. At the time, it was the highest value ever set by an insurance company for a painting. The Louvre museum would eventually elect to spend the money on security instead.

December

16th John Paul Scott became the first person confirmed to have escaped from the prison on Alcatraz Island a to have made it to the California mainland. Scott and Carl D. Parker had sawed through prison bars, and then plunged into the San Francisco Bay with homemade flotation devices, but both became victims of hypothermia in the chilly December waters. Parker gave up after swimming 100 yards and came to shor at the western end of the island. Scott swam three miles and was exhausted and freezing when he was found on the beach by two children.

19th The Mona Lisa arrived in the United States for the first time, as cargo on board the S.S. France. After the Da Vinci masterpiece was unloaded at the French Line Pier in New York City, it was placed into a panel truck and driven to the National Gallery in Washington, D.C. as part of a motorcade that included seven cars.

22nd The "Big Freeze" began in Britain. There would be no frost-free nights until the 5th March 1963.

24th Cuba released the last 1,113 participants from Brigade 2506 in the Bay of Pigs Invasion to the U.S., in exchange for food worth $53 million. The final flight for Operation Ransom arrived at the Homestead AF at 9:00 pm.

25th The Niña II, a replica of the smallest of the three ships that Christopher Columbus had brought to the Ne World in 1492, arrived at the Bahamas' San Salvador Island after a voyage that took 47 days longer than the original trip. Captain Carlos Etayo and a crew of 8 had set off from the Spanish port at Palos de la Frontera on the 19th September with the goal of retracing Columbus's route with hopes of finishing on t 12th October but had not left the Canary Islands until the 10th October, then were not heard from for fif days. Columbus had sailed from Spain to the Bahamas in 70 days, between the 3rd August and 12th Octo 1492.

27th Astronomer Maarten Schmidt made the first visual identification of a quasar, aiming the telescope of th Palomar Observatory in California at 3C 273, visible from Earth within the constellation Virgo.

28th U.S. President Kennedy replied to Soviet Premier Khrushchev's 19th December letter, rejecting the idea (no more than three on-site inspections of nuclear facilities each year. Khrushchev would say later that " had been led to believe", by negotiator Arthur Dean, that the U.S. would settle for three or four per yea while Kennedy said that Dean had mentioned between 8 and 10. No inspections would take place at all until 1988.

29th An Airnautic airliner from France crashed into Monte Renoso on the island of Corsica as it was approach the airport at Ajaccio, killing all 25 people on board. The French investigation determined that the error: by the crew had caused the accident.

30th American oceanographer Albert Oshiver became the first person to ever swim from one end of the Panama Canal to the other, swimming non-stop from Gatun to Gamboa in 29 hours. Oshiver was charge 4-cent toll for the privilege of using the shortcut between the Atlantic and Pacific Oceans, "the smallest ever collected at the Panama Canal".

31st The body of 23-year-old Patricia Bissette was found in her apartment. She was the seventh victim of Alb DeSalvo, the "Boston Strangler". DeSalvo would later confess that he had gotten the name of Bissette's roommate from the mailbox and had posed as the roommate's friend to gain entry.

PEOPLE IN POWER

Robert Menzies
1949-1966
Australia
Prime Minister

Charles de Gaulle
1959-1969
France
Président

João Goulart
1961-1964
Brazil
President

John Diefenbaker
1957-1963
Canada
Prime Minister

Mao Zedong
1943-1976
China
Government of China

Heinrich Lübke
1959-1969
Germany
President of Germany

Rajendra Prasad
1950-1962
India
1st President of India

Giovanni Gronchi
1955-1962
Italy
President

Hiroito
1926-1989
Japan
Emperor

Adolfo López Mateos
1958-1964
Mexico
President of Mexico

Nikita Khrushchev
1958-1964
Russia
Premier

Hendrik Verwoerd
1958-1966
South Africa
Prime Minister

John F. Kennedy
1961-1963
United States
President

Théo Lefèvre
1961-1965
Belgium
Prime Minister

Keith Holyoake
1960-1972
New Zealand
Prime Minister

Harold Macmillan
1957-1963
United Kingdom
Prime Minister

Tage Erlander
1946-1969
Sweden
Prime Minister

Viggo Kampmann
1960-1962
Denmark
Prime Minister

Francisco Franco
1936-1975
Spain
President

János Kádár
1961-1965
Hungary
Hungarian Working
People's Party

Printed in Great Britain
by Amazon

60853231R00048